Women's Wicked Wit

Women's Wicked Wit

from Jane Austen
to Roseanne Barr

MICHELLE LOVRIC

CHICAGO
REVIEW
PRESS

Library of Congress Cataloging-in-Publication Data

Women's wicked wit : from Jane Austen to Roseanne Barr / [compiled by]
Michelle Lovric.

    p. cm

    Originally published: London : Prion Books, 2000.

    ISBN 1-55652-387-4

      1. Women—Quotations. 2. American wit and humor. 3. English wit
    and humor. I. Lovric, Michelle.

PN6081.5 .W585 2001

305.4—dc21   00-048643

Grateful acknowledgment is made to the following for permission to
reprint extracts from copyrighted material: *The Letters of Edith Sitwell*,
reproduced with permission of Virago. Copyright © Edith Sitwell.

Cover design: Bob Eames
Cover photograph: *The Cheat with the Ace of Diamonds*, c. 1635–40
(oil on canvas) by Georges de la Tour (1593–1652), Louvre, Paris,
France/Peter Willi/Bridgeman Library

Printed in Great Britain

Contents

Women on Women	1
Women on Men	5
The Sex War	27
Love	41
Sex	57
Marriage & Divorce	67
Happy Families	91
Who Needs Enemies?	104
Bimbos, Himbos & Bluestockings	113
Brief Encounters	127
Hollywood & Beyond	133
Hisdemeanours & Missdemeanours	151
Bad Behaviour	169
Conspicuous Consumption	189
Food, Fat & Dieting	197
Appearances	209
Work, Power & Money	237
The Arts	251
Sport	260
Animals	265
People & Places	271
Having the Vapours	289
RIP	297

The wit of women is like the airy froth of champagne, or the witching irridescence of the soap-bubble, blown for a moment's sport.
Kate Sanborn

When a man gives his opinion he's a man. When a woman gives her opinion she's a bitch.
Bette Davis

Fighting is essentially a masculine idea; a woman's weapon is her tongue.
Hermione Gingold

A woman's tongue is a tried and trusted jape with men, but it is our substitute for a fist.
Rachel Ferguson

A woman's tongue is a deadly weapon and the most difficult thing in the world to keep in order, and things slip off it with a facility nothing short of appalling.
Elizabeth von Arnim

Women
on Women

Women on Women

I hate Women. They get on my Nerves.

Dorothy Parker

Women unless they are squaws, are as over-individual and untameable as cats.

Margot Asquith

"Whim" is the plural of woman.

Kathy Lette

A girl is a girl. It's nice to be told you're successful at it.

Rita Hayworth

To be somebody, a woman does not have to be more like a man, but has to be more of a woman.

Sally E. Shaywitz

The Victorian ladies lived in a period filled with soothing fictions ... they managed to believe in chastity as an end in itself, even while they were considering its market value.

Doris Langley Moore

I think that women had to suffer this crisis of identity, which began a hundred years ago, and have to suffer it still today, simply to become fully human.

Betty Friedan

Why are women ... so much more interesting to men than men are to women?

Virginia Woolf

And I always went with the boys. Girls seemed a foolish investment of my time.

Mae West

We can very well class women into three distinct root types, from which further amalgamations branch off: The Lover-women — the Mother-women — and the Neuter-women.

Elinor Glyn

There are two categories of women. Those who are women and those who are men's wives.

Charlotte Whitton

Women as women are a luxury, and a luxury that, unlike most others, is too plentiful.

Doris Langley Moore

All women have one gorilla arm. That's the one we use to hold the purse and the kids, reach for the back zipper and protect the front seat.

Diane Nichols

Ask a man if you need help clearing the table. He'll plunk the plates on the first clear surface and leave. Women hang around being helpful and hiding things.

Peg Bracken

Just as women's bodies are softer than men's, so their understanding is sharper.

Christine de Pisan

Wit in women is apt to have bad consequences; like a sword without a scabbard, it wounds the wearer and provokes assailants. I am sorry to say the generality of women who have excelled in wit have failed in chastity.

Elizabeth Montagu

A woman in this age is considered learned enough if she can distinguish her husband's bed from that of another.

Hannah Woolley

From birth to age eighteen, a girl needs good parents. From eighteen to thirty-five, she needs good looks. From thirty-five to fifty-five, she needs a good personality. From fifty-five on, she needs good cash.

Sophie Tucker

What had I known of female character previously to my arrival at Brussels? Precious little. And what was my notion of it? Something vague, slight, gauzy, glittering. Now when I came in contact with it I found it to be a palpable substance enough — very hard too sometimes, and often heavy. There was metal in it, both lead and iron.

Charlotte Brontë

Women
on Men

Women on Men

It is a truth universally acknowledged that one of the most significant problems of modern western society is the male of the species.

Melanie Phillips

Men are my kind of people.

Mae West

Listen, if it's got four wheels or a dick you're goin' a have trouble with it, guaranteed.

Annie Proulx

There are so many kinds of awful men —
One can't avoid them all.

Wendy Cope

I despise men profoundly and from conviction.

Marie Bashkirtseff

There are only two kinds of men — the dead and the deadly.

Helen Rowland

Men are luxuries, not necessities.

Cher

Sometimes I think that if there was a third sex men wouldn't get so much as a glance from me.

Amanda Vail

Maleness remains a recessive genetic trait like colour-blindness and haemophilia.

Elizabeth Gould Davis

Why are we supposed to be with men, anyway? I feel like I used to know.

Lorrie Moore

I believe in women. Men are just unsubstantiated rumours.

Erika Ritter

It's not a bit of use being heavenly with men.

Pearl May Teresa Craigie

Doesn't it feel like you live on the Planet of the Guys?

Kate Clinton

My mother's two categories; nice men did things for you, bad men did things to you.

Margaret Atwood

Boys are always worse.

Elizabeth Hawes

There's nineteen men living in my neighbourhood
There's nineteen men living in my neighbourhood
Eighteen of them are fools and the one ain't no doggone good.

Bessie Smith

For one man's chin is as rough as another's, and one man's lies are as smooth as another's.

Helen Rowland

In what way is a man more than a mango?
Is he more useful about the house?
Will your children like him as much as they'd like a mango?

Lucy Ellmann

Well, I've finally figured out that being male is the same thing, more or less, as having a personality disorder.

Carol Shields

His mother should have thrown him away and kept the stork.

Mae West

To rephrase Samuel Butler, a man is simply a woman's way of making another woman.

Naomi Segal

It's not the men in my life that counts, it's the life in my men.

Mae West

When God created man she was only experimenting.

Graffiti

Bloody men are like bloody buses.

Wendy Cope

8

I don't know how men are different from hogs ... They chase after the same things: food, drink, women.

Emilia Pardo Bazán

Most single men don't even live like people. They live like bears with furniture.

Rita Rudner

Men button dresses the way they load a gun or something, no nonsense about it.

Peg Bracken

I'd like to get to the point where I can be just as mediocre as a man.

Juanita Kreps

Women want mediocre men, and men are working hard to be as mediocre as possible.

Margaret Mead

Wealth makes them lavish, wit knavish, beauty effeminate, poverty deceitful, and deformity ugly. Therefore, of me take this counsel: Esteem of men as of a broken reed, Mistrust them still, and then you well shall speed.

Jane Anger

Every man I meet is a locomotive chimney. Smoke — smoke — smoke — smoke ...

Fanny Fern

There are those who maintain that a man can do everything better than a woman can do it. This is certainly true of nagging. When a man nags he shows his thoroughness, his continuity, and that love of sport which is the special pride and attribute of his sex.

Sarah Grand

Men are perfectly good. The trouble is that they are only good for one thing at a time.

Michelle Lovric

Men are really out to save their own hides, I swear. It's the women who are taking all the risks.

Laura Chester

Man is indeed an amazing piece of mechanism when you see — so to speak — the full weakness — of what he calls — his strength. There is not a female child above the age of eight but might rebuke him for the spoilt petulance of his wilful nonsense.

Charlotte Brontë

Dullards, malingerers, gigolos, sycophants, boors — and that's the best of them ... betrayers all. None of them worth the socks they stick their big feet into.

Lucy Ellmann

She did not rate herself very high, but she rated men lower.

Countess Barcynska

Men think they're more important than women because
their suit jackets have secret pockets on the inside.

Rita Rudner

The natural woman loves and understands man far too well
ever to wish to borrow his position, his work, his trousers.
She sees through his hollow affectation of importance, and
envies him not the proud but unpleasant tasks of earning the
daily bread, filling up the census-paper, carrying the rugs,
and paying the taxes. She has for him the pity which is akin
to love. She knows his clothes don't look half so nice as hers
do, and that without her he is a poor, weak, miserable,
buttonless creature.

Mrs Fanny Douglas

Lo! What a paradox is man — even a puzzle which worketh
backward!

Helen Rowland

We value them too much, and our selves too little, if we
place any part of our worth in their Opinion; and do not
think our selves capable of Nobler Things than the pitiful
Conquest of some worthless heart.

Mary Astell

All men are children, and if you understand that, a woman
understands everything.

Coco Chanel

Only a man can install routine.

Enid Bagnold

If there is anything disagreeable going on, men are sure to get out of it.

Jane Austen

MEN'S MINDS

I have wallowed with the vermin, so I know men's minds.

Mary 'Mother' Jones

Until Eve gave him the apple, [Adam] didn't even know he wasn't wearing underpants.

Paula Yates

I sometimes think that if our world ever goes up in smoke, it will not be because of man's Machiavellian evil, but rather his affable incompetence.

Helen Hayes

Man is a hunter — a hunter always. He may be a poor thing and hunt only a few puny aims ... But he is always hunting, hunting — something — always.

Elinor Glyn

I fear nothing so much as a man who is witty all day long.

Marie de Sévigné

One cannot be always laughing at a man without now and then stumbling on something witty.

Jane Austen

This is the man who, as far as inventions go, thinks
Wonderbra and La Perla are up there with the wheel.

Jane Moore

Women speak because they wish to speak, whereas a man
speaks only when driven to speech by something outside
himself — like, for instance, he can't find any clean socks.

Jean Kerr

Under thirty-five a man has too much to learn, and I don't
have time to teach him.

Hedy Lamarr

Men are not stupid, or at least not too stupid to realize that if
they didn't get sensitive real fast, they weren't going to get
laid anymore.

Cynthia Heimel

He had given her many opportunities to look into him, at
the end of each of his vistas there was something terrifyingly
like a blank wall.

Gertrude Atherton

Unless one could cure men of being fools, it is to no purpose
to cure them of any folly, as it is only making room for some
other.

Anne Mathews

I don't like men of Action without thought. Action must be interpenetrated with Imagination to be remembered. If not it is like a Bull in a China Shop, or perhaps even a Donkey in a Parlour.

Lady Ottoline Morrell

He had a mental palate which would never learn to distinguish between railway tea and nectar.

Edith Wharton

All men are unreasonable; it is their normal state.

Anne Mathews

I am tired of being a free finishing school for men.

Suzanne Wolstenholme

Estimated from a wife's experience, the average man spends fully one-quarter of his life in looking for his shoes.

Helen Rowland

And their hobbies! … Why? Why? Only a man could think that getting a miniature plane off the ground was time well spent.

Lucy Ellmann

Men can read maps better than women. Cause only the male mind could conceive of one inch equalling a hundred miles.

Roseanne Barr

You can talk to a man about any subject. He won't understand, but you can talk to him.

Anonymous

I don't mind the canvas of a man's mind being good, if only it is completely hidden by the worsted and the floss.

Harriet, Lady Ashburton

Courtesans used to know more about the soul of men than any philosopher. The art is lost in the fog of snobbism and false respectability.

Elsa Schiaparelli

Pleasure, to a man of an enquiring mind, means a toad inside a stone, or a beetle running with its head off.

Anne Mathews

Because he has such respect for your superior wisdom and technical know-how, he is constantly asking questions like "Does this kid need a sweater?" or "Is the baby wet?"

Jean Kerr

Only a divinity could determine which is funnier, Man's Dream of Woman, or Woman as she is.

Miriam Beard

The man who pronounces thirty stupidities will nonetheless win the prize on account of his beard.

Marie de Gournay

Men have to learn things that women have known for centuries.
Toni Halliday

A retentive memory is of great use to a man, no doubt; but the talent of oblivion is on the whole more useful.
Ouida

VIOLENCE

Perhaps the predilection of men for rapine and slaughter should be interpreted as meaning that men are premenstrual at all times.
Germaine Greer

Nuclear bombs, fluorescent lights, burning witches at the stake, deciding animals have no emotions — only men could have come up with such ideas.
Lucy Ellmann

Man with his artificial things he keeps inventing; false birds which are our airplanes, false whales that are our submarines, and now a false end of the world that is the atom bomb.
Genêt

Men are so ethical, they let us die for their principles!
Lucy Ellmann

Only a male is competent to deal with a bazooka; he made it up. He made it up because another man invented a tank; he made it up because another earlier man invented machine guns.
Genêt

Men are beasts and even beasts don't behave as they do.
Brigitte Bardot

All men are rapists and that's all they are. They rape us with their eyes, their laws and their codes.
Marilyn French

THE MALE EGO

Beneath the thick skin of the stronger sex lies an open wound called the Male Ego.
Letty Cottin Pogrebin

The male ego with few exceptions is elephantine to start with.
Bette Davis

A man's modesty ... is nearly always more delicate, more sincere than ours.
Colette

Nine out of ten males will believe anything, especially if it confirms their virility.
Andrea Martin

Beware of men who cry. It's true that men who cry are sensitive and in touch with feelings, but the only feelings they tend to be sensitive to and in touch with are their own.
Nora Ephron

Women on Men

I was wrong in believing there was a man capable of hiding what pleases his vanity.

Marie de la Fayette

Old men are like that, you know. It makes them feel important to think that they are in love with somebody.

Willa Cather

Women have served all these centuries as looking-glasses possessing the magic and delicious power of reflecting the figure of man at twice its natural size.

Virginia Woolf

They say men enjoy shaving — it's the one time each day they get to look in the mirror and say, "Hey there, you handsome devil!"

Helen Gurley Brown

He was like a cock who thought the sun had risen to hear him crow.

George Eliot

Research has shown that men usually sleep on the right side of the bed. Even in their sleep they have to be right.

Rita Rudner

On stage there can be slight problems if the leading man is more feminine than the leading woman.

Joan Rivers

But men are weak and constantly need reassurance, so now that they fail to find adulation in the opposite sex, they're turning to each other.

Anita Loos

Strange how blind self-love renders you men; were you not wholly absorbed in a partial admiration of your own abilities, you would long since have acknowledged the force of what I am now going to urge.

Judith Sargent Murray

Men normally take most pleasure in spreading bad news, because it makes them feel important.

Elsa Schiaparelli

Praise is better than wheatgerm for even the least vain of men.

Phyllis McGinley

What say we reduce men to their normal size so that they'll fit into our life?

Cynthia Heimel

Men, though, have still got this ludicrous, operatic solemnity about their "manhood", and not being made a "woman" of. So they bottle it up, and it makes them ugly.

Julie Burchill

A bachelor never quite gets over the idea that he is a thing of beauty and a boy forever.

Helen Rowland

Women on Men

Who needs yesterday's paper, who needs yesterday's man?

Julie Burchill

What's so special about Christmas — the birth of a man who thinks he's a god isn't such a rare event.

Graffiti

AS LOVERS

I sometimes think that what men really want now is a sexually experienced virgin.

Anonymous

A man may feel like a brute at taking a kiss from a nice girl — but it isn't until after he's gotten the kiss.

Helen Rowland

It's not that men fear intimacy ... it's that they're hypochondriacs of intimacy: They always think they have it when they don't.

Lorrie Moore

In my opinion, a man is a Man if he is good at sex.

Julie Burchill

There are men for whom complication sums up the very image of love.

Gabrielle Chanel

[Some guys] make love like they were the only ones in the room, which I think is a holdover from when they were.

Diane Nichols

They are born to deceive, to deprive, to misunderstand, mislead, ignore and ruin women. Love is wasted, wasted on them.

Lucy Ellmann

A woman is a woman until the day she dies, but a man's a man only as long as he can.

Jackie "Moms" Mabley

THAT USELESS PIECE OF FLESH

Q: What's that useless piece of flesh at the end of a penis called?
A: A Man.

Graffiti

Feminism exists to decentre the power of the phallus as political instrument of magic.

Naomi Segal

Why should we give penises any more respect than, oh, earlobes? Are we supposed to worship it, revere it, make it into some kind of mystical being?

Cynthia Heimel

Women on Men

We've never been in a democracy, we've always been in a phallocracy!

Françoise Parturier

Men have always detested women's gossip because they suspect the truth: their measurements are being taken and compared.

Erica Jong

Fast vehicles, bombs, male bonding were called into service to allay his persistent phallic anxiety.

Germaine Greer

It is not just there to look pretty, a thing it is very bad at anyway.

Julie Burchill

I think men are very funny. If I had one of those dangly things stuffed down the front of my pants, I'd sit at home all day laughing at myself.

Dawn French

A delicately rosy, silky-satin, somehow innocent, always-vulnerable erect penis is probably the most fascinating object in the world.

Helen Gurley Brown

Show me a frigid woman and, nine times out of ten, I'll show you a little man.

Julie Burchill

Beware of the man who denounces woman writers; his penis is tiny & cannot spell.

Erica Jong

Do we want one? Good God, no! The day Freud came up with penis envy, I think his brains had to have been out to lunch.

Helen Gurley Brown

I have a little bit of penis envy. Yeah, they're ridiculous, but they're cool.

k. d. lang

We have no envy. I don't care what the misguided patriarch Sigmund Freud said. We may like a penis, but we don't want one.

Cynthia Heimel

I mean, if you were a bloke, would you put it in a mouth, where there are teeth? The teeth of a female who's been discriminated against for centuries?

Kathy Lette

I do not give blow jobs. Why not? Because I find it really off-putting, seeing a grown man look that pathetically grateful.

Jenny Eclair

INDIVIDUALS

Dean Swift, by his lordship's own account, was so intoxicated
with the love of flattery, he sought it amongst the lowest of
people, and the silliest of women; and was never so well
pleased with any companions, as those that worshipped him,
while he insulted them ...

Lady Mary Wortley Montagu

Was there a star in the East when this self-worshipping little
man was born?

Jean Rook on Eric Morley, organizer of the Miss World competition

Valerie Solanas had to shoot her man to get him to take
more than patronizing notice of her.

Germaine Greer

And David Diddy Hamilton has sworn — forcibly — never
to speak to me again, since I described his "bright, shiny
personality, his ego twice as long as his arms, and that hair-do
which makes him look like a newly-thatched cottage".

Jean Rook

He is just about the nastiest little man I've ever known. He
struts sitting down.

Lillian K. Dykestra on Thomas Dewey

Reddin of Undern cared as little for the graciousness of life
as he did for its pitiful rhapsodies, its purple-mantled
tragedies. He had no time for such trivialities.

Mary Webb

Oh, and an excellent thing it is; I make Philistine rub Sir Sampson every morning and night. If it was not for that, and his cough, nobody would know whether he were dead or alive; I don't believe he would know himself — humph!

Susan Ferrier

He is a hanger-on of rich young men. He shows them life. He wins their money — and like that other hanger-on, the leech, he drops away from them when he is gorged and they are empty. Can you choose the daughter of such a man for your wife?

Mary Braddon

Poor little man. They made him out of lemon Jell-O and there he is.

Adela Rogers St John on Robert Redford

His spirit is made of pap, his body of chewed string, and his heart a pumpkin fricasseed in snow.

Ninon de Lenclos, regarding Charles de Sévigné

Fang told me that he was a self-made man. It wasn't until later that I discovered that he would have been wise to get some help.

Phyllis Diller on her stage husband, "Fang"

It beats me how Freud could say "What do women want?" as if we must all want the same things.

Katharine Whitehorn

Women on Men

At least some of the men who write sex books admit that they really don't understand female sexuality. Freud was one. Masters is another — that was why he got Johnson.

Arlene Croce

Charlie Chaplin fancies himself a great lover, but I fancy him as a great coward ... I bow to his talent, which verges on genius. Would that his character matched it.

Hedda Hopper

In the picture of our century, as taken from life by History, this very man should have been a central figure; but now, owing to his want of steadfastness, there will be for ever a blur where Brougham should have been.

Harriet Martineau on Lord Brougham and Vaux

The Sex War

The Sex War

If you're a woman living, you've been done wrong by a man.
Oprah Winfrey

If they could put one man on the moon, why can't they put them all?

Anonymous

Why can't men get more in touch with their feminine side and become self-destructive?
Betsy Salkind

You mean the poisonous man-hating shrew syndrome. Lord, yes.
Dolly Parton

I don't think men and women are meant to live together. They are totally different animals.
Diana Dors

If you're a woman — and who isn't these days? — you know where the real fight for equality and justice is taking place ... in the bathrooms of America.
Alice Kahn

To write, or read, or think, or to inquire,
Would cloud our beauty, and exhaust our time,
And interrupt the conquests of our prime,
Whilst the dull manage of a servile house
Is held by some our utmost art and use.
Anne Finch, Countess of Winchelsea

The Sex War

It's funny about men and women. Men pay in cash to get them and to get rid of them. Women, on the other hand, pay emotionally coming and going. Neither has it easy.

Hedy Lamarr

I have had my belly full of great men (forgive the expression). I quite like to read about them in the pages of Plutarch, where they don't outrage my humanity. Let us see them carved in marble or cast in bronze, and hear no more about them. In real life they are nasty creatures, persecutors, temperamental, despotic, bitter and suspicious.

George Sand

Old men, young men, boys. Pah! They fill me with repulsion. There is nothing in the world more repellant to me, even small boys I think unutterably repellant.

Violet Keppel

In passing, also, I would like to say that the first time Adam had a chance he laid the blame on woman.

Nancy Astor

But remember, a man ends by hating the woman who he thinks has found him out.

Jennie Jerome Churchill

When a girl refuses to kiss a man he is never disconcerted; he is merely astonished that she could be so blind to her own feelings.

Helen Rowland

The Sex War

Women fail to understand how much men hate them.

Germaine Greer

What men say about women is generally wrong. What they think and don't say is far more correct.

Diana Woods

I think women have a different spirituality to men. We share the same emotions basically, but social structures always have been set up by men ... Even Tampax is made by men.

k. d. lang

When a man can't explain a woman's actions, the first thing he thinks about is the condition of her uterus.

Clare Boothe Luce

A woman need know but one man well, in order to understand all men; whereas a man may know all women and understand not one of them.

Helen Rowland

Vain man is apt to think we were merely intended for the World's propagation, and to keep its human inhabitants sweet and clean; but by their leaves, had we the same Literature, he would find our brains as fruitful as our bodies.

Hannah Woolley

Lo, an intelligent opinion in the mouth of a woman horrifieth a man even as the scissors in the mouth of a babe.

Helen Rowland

Whatever women do they must do twice as well as men to be thought half as good. Luckily, this is not difficult.

Charlotte Whitton

Why is it that *The Oxford Dictionary of Quotations* bulges with quotations by men ... when women (as men are the first to point out) do all the talking?

Peg Bracken

A man can never understand how a woman gets so much joy out of leading him all the way to the threshold of love and then sweetly closing the door in his face.

Helen Rowland

Of anything that could be called mind in a woman Tony had a dislike which was akin to absolute fear.

Mary Braddon

Many militant women show too plainly by their inefficiency, their obesity and their belligerence, that they have not succeeded in finding any measure of liberation in their own company.

Germaine Greer

The New Woman reminds me of an agriculturalist who, discarding a fine farm of his own, and leaving it to nettles, stones, thistles, and wire-worms, should spend his whole time in demanding neighbouring fields which are not his.

Ouida

The Sex War

The only difference between men and women is that women are able to create new little human beings in their bodies while ... doing everything men do.

Erica Jong

No man can understand why a woman should prefer a good reputation to a good time.

Helen Rowland

Men do not look at a woman with women's eyes. Men, being three parts animal themselves, condone any offence in a woman the animal part of whom is perfect and beautiful.

Rhoda Broughton

He accused me of the thing men think is the most insulting thing they can accuse you of — wanting to be married.

Nora Ephron

In her world, men loved women as the fox loves the hare. And women loved men as the tapeworm loves the gut.

Pat Barker

Are you my alternative?
Florynce R. Kennedy to a male heckler who asked if she was a lesbian

Men are judged as the sum of their parts while women are judged as some of their parts.

Julie Burchill

The Sex War

Ever since Eve gave Adam the apple, there has been a misunderstanding between the sexes about gifts.

Nan Robertson

I'm furious about the Women's Liberationists ... proclaiming that women are brighter than men. That's true, but it should be kept very quiet or it ruins the whole racket.

Anita Loos

It occurred to me when I was thirteen and wearing white gloves and Mary Janes and going to dancing school, that no one should have to dance backwards all their lives.

Jill Ruckelshaus

The major concrete achievement of the women's movement in the 1970s was the Dutch treat.

Nora Ephron

A woman's body is the politician's vessel, to be used and regulated as the political climate demands.

Barbara Howars

Don't let a man put anything over you except an umbrella.

Mae West

Many men admire strong women, but they do not love them.

Elsa Schiaparelli

The Sex War

Is it to be understood that the principles of the Declaration of Independence bear no relation to half of the human race?

Harriet Martineau

But if God wanted us to think with our wombs, why did He give us a brain?

Clare Boothe Luce

I don't need a man to rectify my existence. The most profound relationship we'll ever have is the one with ourselves.

Shirley MacLaine

A woman without a man is like a neck without a pain.

Graffiti

A woman without a man is like a fish without a bicycle.

Gloria Steinem

If you catch a man, throw him back.

Women's liberation slogan

People say I've set back the women's movement thirty years.

Madonna

Well if woman upset the world, do give her a chance to set it right side up again.

Sojourner Truth

I had explained that a woman's asking for equality in the church would be comparable to a black person's demanding equality in the Ku Klux Klan.

Mary Daly

The problem of feminism was and remains men.

Naomi Segal

We cannot reduce women to equality. Equality is a step down for most women.

Phyllis Schlafly

The poor men seem to be all in confusion, and don't know what to do. Why children, if you have woman's rights give it to her and you will feel better. You will have your own rights, and they won't be so much trouble.

Sojourner Truth

All this Women's Liberation noise, I'm for it, of course — what I'm against is their idea that they invented it.

Katharine Hepburn

As long as some men use physical force to subjugate females, all men need not. The knowledge that some men do suffices to threaten all women.

Marilyn French

"Strong Woman", used by men, means "she can take it". And if she can take it, why not do it to her again?

Julie Burchill

The Sex War

Naive conclusions to draw from man's brutality! Because man is a brute, woman has to be locked up so that she will remain unharmed.

Hedwig Dohm

Legislation and case law still exist in some parts of the US permitting the "passion shooting" by a husband of a wife; the reverse, of course, is known as homicide.

Diane B. Schulder

It is not necessary to beat up a woman to beat her down.

Marilyn French

There's more than one way to brutalize a woman.

Laura Chester

The woman who pins her faith to a man won't find a safety-pin strong enough to stand the strain.

Helen Rowland

[Men] have realized, as we have forgotten, that you can get people saddled with almost any amount of work so long as you disguise it as any amount of power.

Katharine Whitehorn

A woman who is a wife is one who has made a permanent sex bargain for her maintenance; the woman who is not married must therefore make a temporary bargain of the same kind.

Christabel Pankhurst

Men do not rest easy in their graves unless they have deprived every woman they have ever come into contact with of whatever she wanted from them.

Lucy Ellmann

I've no time for broads who want to rule the world alone. Without men, who'd do up the zipper on the back of your dress?

Bette Davis

A career woman who has survived the hurdle of marriage and maternity encounters a new obstacle: the hostility of men.

Caroline Bird

Men are afraid of me.

Grace Jones

Barely have I encountered in a woman the kind of hostility with which a man regards the mistresses who have exploited him sexually. The woman, on the contrary, knows herself to be an almost inexhaustible store of plenty for the man.

Colette

Burning dinner is not incompetence but war.

Marge Piercy

SCUM Society for Cutting Up Men Manifesto
Valerie Solanas — book title

Women should care a bit less so that men are made to care a bit more.

Jill Tweedie's fictional character, Martha the Fainthearted Feminist

Men who consistently leave the toilet seat up secretly want women to get up to go to the bathroom in the middle of the night and fall in.

Rita Rudner

From when I was very young I just knew that being a girl and being charming in a feminine sort of way could get me a lot of things, and I milked it for everything I could.

Madonna

His convictions told him that women are people, but his impulses told him they're not, really.

Lucille Kallen

Men punish and carve up the most passionate, the truest, the noblest sentiments experienced by women, and among themselves they only boast of smut. What lies in store for us women in the society of the future? Who can say? The present state of things is a long martyrdom.

Louise Colet

Most women set out to try to change a man, and when they have changed him they do not like him.

Marlene Dietrich

Poor Mary Ann! She gave the guy an inch and now he thinks he's a ruler.

Mae West

The vote, I thought, means nothing to women. We should be armed.

Edna O'Brien

When they find themselves confronted with utter unreasonableness, perversity, and erratic curvatures of temper, they solve the problem with a baby, and pass on.

Gertrude Atherton

If ever the struggle becomes grandiose and bloody I wish to partake of it, I wish to unite all women, all mothers, all these sisters in pain and misery, and make them understand what must be said, what must be done, what must be demanded! … To keep them from eternally remaining machines for pleasure and for the reproduction of the species! Until then I shall steep myself in solitude and meditation.

Louise Colet

The way to a man's heart is through his heart and it helps if it hurts. Hurts him, not you.

Doris Lilly

You can bind my body, tie my hands, govern my actions: you are the strongest, and society adds to your power; but with my will, sir, you can do nothing.

George Sand

Love

Love

If love is the answer, can you rephrase the question?

Lily Tomlin

What is it that love does to a woman?

Ouida

Love is something sent from Heaven to worry the hell out of you.

Dolly Parton

Once begun, a love affair is like a train headed through a tunnel.

Helen Gurley Brown

The third age of love is the callow age, in which a boy always falls in love with a woman old enough to be his mother. It is accompanied by a desire on his part to be thought very, very old, and very, very wicked.

Dorothy Dix

Every extra day is one less day when one does not love.

Marlene Dietrich

When in love, I become a geisha, as dirty and as pure as that implies.

Julie Burchill

We all love in sizes.

Djuna Barnes

Can love be calm, resigned, free from desire? Impetuous only a few days a year and relegated the rest of the time to a compartment in the brain?

Louise Colet

Love: woman's eternal spring and man's eternal fall.

Helen Rowland

Sometimes I believe that some people are better at love than others, and sometimes I believe that everyone is faking it.

Nora Ephron

For love to last, you had to have illusions or have no illusions at all. But you had to stick to one or the other. It was the switching back and forth that endangered things.

Lorrie Moore

Being in love was like running barefoot along a street covered with broken bottles.

Margaret Atwood

Love becomes the deposit of the heart, analogous in all degrees to the "findings" in a tomb.

Djuna Barnes

Is love a curse or a blessing? I sometimes think it is like death. A strange comparison you will say. But, like death, it is a doorway we go through blindfold, whether we will or not; the bandage falls from our eyes, and we find ourselves in heaven or hell.

Mrs W. K. Clifford

Love

It is impossible for the dispassionate observer to understand what people see in each other.

Alice Thomas Ellis

A loving heart has a cataract and cannot see.

Louise Colet

When people are in love, they are in a magnetic state, and are very much astonished at themselves when they come to their senses.

Geraldine Endsor Jewsbury

Love is not merely blind but mentally afflicted.

Alice Thomas Ellis

In my experience, pride is a word often on women's lips — but they display little sign of it where love affairs are concerned.

Agatha Christie

I have never met anybody who has been made as happy by love as he has been made sad.

Alice Thomas Ellis

Climate and idleness have much to do with certain manifestations of what is classed, very erroneously, as love.

Elinor Glyn

Falling in love is no way of getting to know someone.

Sheila Sullivan

Dear, where we love much we always forgive, because we ourselves are nothing, and what we love is all.

Ouida

Were I sarcastic, I would say misfortune and love are synonymous.

Marie Bashkirtseff

I'm miserable if I'm not in love and, of course, I'm miserable if I am.

Tallulah Bankhead

Every little girl knows about love. It is only her capacity to suffer because of it that increases.

Françoise Sagan

Trust has nothing to do with love. It's vigilance that's important.

Marlene Dietrich

You know, new lovers really should have a minimum isolation period of say, six months, so as not to nauseate absolutely everyone they meet.

Kathy Lette

Falling in love is a condition, keeping in love an art ... some women who have been masters of their art have been loved to the coffin's edge.

Mary Garden

Love

What we say about love and what we do about love are generally two different things.

Rita Mae Brown

A youth with his first cigar makes himself sick; a youth with his first girl makes other people sick.

Mary Wilson Little

Teasing and tormenting is the sustenance, the breath, the very life, of most young women who are sure of the affections of their lovers.

Jane Collier

How could I be sleeping with this peculiar man ... Surely only true love could justify my lack of taste.

Margaret Atwood

I would hope I can attract both men and women. And that when a person is attracted to me, they're not thinking about my genitals.

k. d. lang

SINGLEDOM

Social graces are dead ... chivalry is dead, tact is dead, game-playing is dead ... Mr Right is dead, manners are dead, prudence is dead, expectations of any kind are dead.

Rona Jaffe

No man wanted me. Rapists would tap me on the shoulder and say, "Seen any girls?"

Joan Rivers

Anatomists will tell you that there is a heart in the withered old maid's carcass, the same as in that of any cherished wife or proud mother in the land. Can this be so? I really don't know, but feel inclined to doubt it.

Charlotte Brontë

A single woman who has never married sometimes wishes she could carry a document around which would verify the fact that at least someone asked her.

Helen Gurley Brown

It is well to love even a dog when you have the opportunity, for fear you should find nothing else worth loving.

Louise Honorine de Choiseul

Girls! Those of you who have hearts, and therefore wish for happiness, homes, and husbands, bye-and-bye, never develop a reputation of being clever. It will put you out of the matrimonial running as effectually as though it had been circulated that you had leprosy.

Miles Franklin

Eventually, people are willing to admit most of their flaws — greed, jealousy, pride, hostility — but the feeling they're most ashamed to admit is loneliness.

Rona Jaffe

Things get better for single people every day. Oh yes. How cheerful to reflect, for example, that *Sainsburys* now sells "Single Bananas" in a special bag.

Lynne Truss

Love

All old maids are perfectionists. That's why they're old maids.

Edna Ferber

DATING

A man in the house is worth two in the street.

Mae West

Sometimes love doesn't come to us. We have to go out hunting. It's like pigs looking for truffles. It's called dating.

Patti LuPone

He wasn't exactly my type, but look where my type had gotten me.

Nora Ephron

Ultimately I had two rather noncombustible beaux during college.

Fannie Hurst

How many of you ever started dating someone because you were too lazy to commit suicide?

Judy Tenuta

No, Mother, I haven't
met Mr Right yet ...
but I have met Mr Cheap,
Mr Rude, and Mr Married.

T-shirt

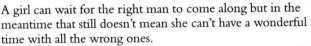

A girl can wait for the right man to come along but in the meantime that still doesn't mean she can't have a wonderful time with all the wrong ones.

Cher

Men, I feel, are like wine — before buying, a real connoisseur takes a small sip and spits them out.

Jill Tweedie's fictional character, Martha the Fainthearted Feminist

POOR MATERIAL

Lo, the woods are full of men, but men are full of strange suspicions; and in elusiveness the fox is simple beside them.

Helen Rowland

I had only one beau in Altoona: a dentist. For a while I dreamed about what marriage to him would be like. But I stopped dreaming one Saturday when we went picnicking and I saw him in a bathing suit. He was covered all over with fur and reminded me of an emaciated orang-outan.

Hedda Hopper

You love like a coward ... Just stand around and hope for things to happen outright. Unthankful and unknowing like a hog under an acorn tree.

Zora Neale Hurston

I'd like to marry a nice domesticated homosexual with a fetish for wiping down formica and different vacuum-cleaner attachments.

Jenny Eclair

Love

Everything in my life that I ever wanted, if I tried for it, I can say I got it, but with men, the harder I tried, the harder I flopped.

Fanny Brice

I am a woman meant for a man, but I never found a man who could compete.

Bette Davis

You get all your boyfriends on sale. It's called Bargain Debasement.

Lorrie Moore

Never trust a man who says "Don't struggle".

Jenny Eclair

The nice men, being nice, hesitate — and in love, as in war, he who hesitates is lost.

Erica Jong

A bachelor is a large body of egotism, completely surrounded by caution and fortified at all points by suspicion.

Helen Rowland

Smoking is the great romance of a lifetime. If I could find someone I wanted forty-five times a day, perhaps I could stop.

Fran Lebowitz

Mostly, men are rottener to women in love than women are to men.

Helen Gurley Brown

"Is this the man whose mind I have married? Is this the man who is to teach me to live by the intellect? Is this the scholar and the sage, whose teaching was to lift me out of the circle of my narrow interests into the sphere of the Universal?" she asks with contemptuous misgivings; "This, whose whole soul is occupied by mean parsimonies, and economies of cheese-rinds and candle-ends?"

Rhoda Broughton

Personally, I can think of nothing more tiresome than being saddled with the kind of weed that sobs and gets sympathy-PMS, or pees sitting down as a sign of "respect" for women.

India Knight

A good man doesn't just happen. They have to be created by us women ... So, first you gotta get rid of all the stuff his mom did to him. And then you gotta get rid of all that macho crap that they pick up from beer commercials.

Roseanne Barr

The heart of a woman is a secret sanctuary where she is constantly burning incense and candles before a succession of idols of clay.

Helen Rowland

There are three kinds of kissers: the fire extinguisher, the mummy and the vacuum cleaner.

Helen Gurley Brown

"Women are like barnacles," he said; "they are always ready to fasten upon a wreck."

Mary Braddon

I have known many a woman to pass through life with a pygmy beside her, taking him for a giant all the while, nor undeceived to the end.

Rhoda Broughton

BAD LOVE EXPERIENCES

There's not a game in the world you can play without the risk of getting hurt some.

Katharine Hepburn

"Don't put all your eggs in one basket," is a proverb which no woman has ever yet learnt, or will ever learn, for from the beginning of time she has put all her eggs in the one frail basket of love.

Norma Lorimer

The longest absence is less perilous to love than the terrible trials of incessant proximity.

Ouida

I don't have a love life. I have a like life.

Lorrie Moore

Romance without finance is a nuisance. Few men value free merchandise.

Sally Stanford

I have been in steady relationships with men since I was eighteen, with not a week off for good behaviour.

Julie Burchill

I have no patience with women who measure and weigh their love like a country doctor dispensing capsules. If a man is worth loving at all, he is worth loving generously, even recklessly.

Marie Dressler

A woman has got to love a bad man once or twice in her life, to be thankful for a good one.

Marjorie Kinnan Rawlings

Save a boyfriend for a rainy day. And another in case it doesn't rain.

Mae West

Love without intimacy, she knew, was an unsung tune. It was all in your head.

Lorrie Moore

Love wears a bumper sticker that says "My other car is a hearse".

Julie Burchill

Gentlemen don't love love. They just like to kick it around.

Sophie Tucker

If only one could tell true love from false love as one can tell mushrooms from toadstools.

Katherine Mansfield

Love

I have concealed as long as I can the uneasiness the nothingness of your letters has given me ... If your inclination is gone I had rather never receive a letter from you than one which in lieu of comfort for your absence gives me a pain even beyond it. For my part, as 'tis my first, this is my last complaint, and your next of that kind shall go back enclosed to you in blank paper.

Lady Mary Wortley Montagu

For me, on a scale of one to ten, romance comes about eighth, after chess but before politics and football.

Alice Thomas Ellis

END OF LOVE

"In love" doesn't make one tender. It makes one furious or jealous, or miserable when it stops.

Enid Bagnold

There's nothing worse than rejection. It's worse than death. I would wish sometimes for the guy to die because at least then I could go to his grave and visit.

Oprah Winfrey

Absence makes the heart grow frantic, not fonder.

Judith Viorst

Where does love go? When something you have taped to the wall falls off, what has happened to the stickum?

Lorrie Moore

A greater love does not kill a smaller one; it only adds pomp to the funeral.

Rona Jaffe

It is the devastating matter-of-factness which kills all romance.

Elinor Glyn

And what, for instance, would have happened had Romeo and Juliet lived to middle age, their silhouettes broadened by pasta?

Anita Loos

Compliments are given with clenched teeth after an affair has ended.

Rona Jaffe

The "Green-Eyed Monster" causes much woe, but the absence of this ugly serpent argues the presence of a corpse whose name is Eros.

Minna Antrimz

When you start having lunch and actually eating, it's already over.

Erica Jong

Every adoration is as seasonal as Christmas.

Lorrie Moore

Love

Lord, I don't think no man love can last
They love you to death then treat you like a thing of the past.

Bessie Smith

The Technique of the Love Affair … If only it had been written
and placed in my hands years ago, maybe I could have been
successful, instead of just successive.

Dorothy Parker

Don't put an absurdly high value on him. Think of the
millions of other girls doing without him, yet able to bear it!

Orfea Sybil

COMPENSATIONS

You don't have a man, you need spaghetti.

Oprah Winfrey

Personally, I think that if a woman hasn't met the right man
by the time she's twenty-four, she may be lucky.

Deborah Kerr

The more I see of men, the more I like dogs.

Germaine de Staël

It's not worth the hassle … My view was, no thanks, actually, I
can take my own kit off at my age.

Helen Stevenson

Sex

Sex is part of nature. I go along with nature.

Marilyn Monroe

Is it all a matter of hormones? Oestrogen *über alles*? Nature gives us thirty years of blindness to male bullshit so we can make the maximum number of babies.

Erica Jong

It was never dirty to me. After all, God gave us the equipment and the opportunity. There's that old saying "If God had meant for us to fly, he'd have given us wings'. Well, look at what he did give us.

Dolly Parton

Sex, which has been acclaimed by too many misguided poets as an utopian activity, seldom attains that status in the human race.

Anita Loos

"Sex," she says, "is a subject like any other subject. Every bit as interesting as agriculture."

Muriel Spark

I find it very difficult to draw a line between what's sex and what isn't. It can be very, very sexy to drive a car, and completely unsexy to flirt with someone at a bar.

Björk Gudmundsdottir

In this age after Freud, sex is immediately suspect.

Betty Friedan

There is an old saying in my family: push sex out of the front door and it will come back through the plughole.

Lynne Truss

There are things that happen in the dark between two people that make everything that happens in the light seem all right.

Erica Jong

Everything in our house has a moral value. Work was an absolute good. Sex was an absolute bad.

Helen Stevenson

Is woman a lost sex? If so, is she the only lost sex?

Elizabeth Hawes

If it happens that you do want peanut butter in bed while you're having sex and your partner doesn't, in the long run the thing to do may be to find another partner.

Dr Ruth Westheimer

Sex is not a sin. Many people have complained that this is taking all the fun out of sex.

Dr Ruth Westheimer

It's impolite to have sex anywhere that is visible to other people who aren't having sex.

Jenny Eclair

Sex

Sex, on the whole, was meant to be short, nasty and brutish.
If what you want is cuddling, you should buy a puppy.

Julie Burchill

When the only place a relationship wholly works is in bed,
both people eventually get nervous ... because they have to
get out of bed.

Erica Jong

If your sexual fantasies were truly of interest to others they
would no longer be fantasies.

Fran Lebowitz

As I look around the West End these days, it seems to me
that outside every thin girl is a fat man, trying to get in.

Katharine Whitehorn

MEN WANT WOMEN MORE THAN WOMEN WANT
MEN. This is simply a fact. This is why men pay for sex and
women don't.

Julie Burchill

When you meet a man, don't you always idly wonder what
he'd be like in bed? I do.

Helen Gurley Brown

How quickly bodies come to love each other, promise
themselves to each other always, without asking permission
from the mind!

Lorrie Moore

I dig skin, lips and Latin men.

Madonna

I was a hedonist long before I knew what a hedonist was.

Tallulah Bankhead

To sum up my attitude to sex, you could say I love everybody, but that doesn't mean I have to make it with them.

Jean Rook

I've never had sex I didn't like.

Dolly Parton

Sex appeal is fifty per cent what you've got, and fifty per cent what people think you've got.

Sophia Loren

LOSING VIRGINITY

To know what's called the facts of life, the breeding arrangements, is nothing. What I was desperate about was the tiny moves.

Enid Bagnold

There are worse motives for having sex the first time than plain curiosity.

Paula Yates

I wouldn't like to sleep with a guy who was a virgin. I'd have to teach him stuff and I don't have the patience.

Madonna

I am pleased, as you may be disappointed, to say that at seventeen I was a virgin. I certainly didn't look like one.

Tallulah Bankhead

When I first found out about how I'd come into the world, I remember longing in my bed at night that I'd been made in a factory not in a bed.

Helen Stevenson

Chastity is comparative, like crime.

Joan Conquest

I didn't lose my virginity until I knew what I was doing.

Madonna

I had promised my soul to Satan if I could have sex with Marc Bolan before I started menstruating.

Julie Burchill

ORAL SEX

The only people any good at cunnilingus are didgeridoo players because they can do circular breathing, which means they can go down on you for about six years. And that's how long it takes.

Jenny Eclair

Some men love oral sex ... If you find a man like this, treat him well. Feed him caviar and don't let your girlfriends catch a glimpse of him.

Cynthia Heimel

NOT GETTING IT

One person's safe sex is another's abstinence.

Alice Kahn

I have this theory that, in five or six years, the virgin will come back like a bomb.

Barbara Cartland

Most husbands who are not making love to their wives are not making love to anybody, black stockings and suspender belts regardless.

Germaine Greer

Men always fall for frigid women because they put on the best show.

Fanny Brice

I used to call us the Three Nuns — can't get none, can't have none, don't meet none.

Sheila Ferguson of The Three Degrees

Losing your real virginity is when you first come with someone, I believe. A bit like the Queen having two birthdays.

Julie Burchill

Believe me, men would fake if they could.

Helen Gurley Brown

There are days when I ask myself whether it's preferable to arouse a man's desire or to satisfy it.

Nicole de Buron

It may be discovered someday that an orgasm actually lasts for hours and only seems like a few seconds.

Dolly Parton

I believe in educating people to be sexual gourmets.

Dr Ruth Westheimer

An orgasm is a way of saying you enjoyed yourself, even as you compliment a host on a wonderful spinach quiche.

Helen Gurley Brown

Being in touch with our Inner Bitch ensures that we will have orgasms. Even with other people.

Elizabeth Hilts

DON'T FEEL LIKE IT

Sex was for men, and marriage, like lifeboats, was for women and children.

Carrie Fisher

The truth was that with all my lipstick and mascara and curves I was as unresponsive as a fossil ... I used to lie awake at night wondering why the boys came after me.

Marilyn Monroe

Phone sex is a growth industry these disease-conscious days. Through the miracle of modern technology, you can reach out and not touch someone.

Alice Kahn

I have never liked bargains when it came to sex.

Hedy Lamarr

I've got two sex speeds: Mad For It and Why Bother?

Julie Burchill

When I had my baby, I screamed and screamed. And that was just during conception.

Joan Rivers

He wondered why sexual shyness, which excites the desire of dissolute women, arouses the contempt of decent ones.

Colette

Marriage
&
Divorce

Marriage and Divorce

Love and marriage go together like angel cake and anthrax.

Julie Burchill

The state of matrimony is a dangerous disease: far better to take drink in my opinion.

Marie de Sévigné

Any intelligent woman who reads the marriage contract, and then goes into it, deserves all the consequences.

Isadora Duncan

In olden time sacrifices were made at the altar — a custom which is still continued.

Helen Rowland

A little weeping, a little wheedling, a little self-degradation, a little careful use of our advantages, and then some man will say: "Come, be my wife!"

Olive Schreiner

The trouble with some women is that they get all excited about nothing — and then they marry him.

Cher

Women who have fostered a romantic unnatural delicacy of feeling, waste their lives in imagining how happy they should have been with a husband who could love them with a fervid increasing affection every day, and all day. But they might as well pine married as single.

Mary Wollstonecraft

I know what I wish Ralph Nader would investigate next. Marriage. It's not safe, it's not safe at all.

Jean Kerr

Oh girls! set your affections on cats, poodles, parrots or lap dogs; but let matrimony alone. It's the hardest way on earth of getting a living.

Fanny Fern

I have been this ten days in debate whether I should hang or marry, in which time I have cried some two hours every day and knocked my head against the wall some fifteen times.

Lady Mary Wortley Montagu

Love-matches are made by people who are content, for a month of honey, to condemn themselves to a life of vinegar.

Marguerite Blessington

Marriage used to be for the having and growing of children; now there are few marriages that can withstand the pressures of those events.

Erica Jong

The early marriages of silly children … where … every woman is married before she well knows how serious a matter human life is …

Harriet Martineau

My boyfriend and I broke up. He wanted to get married, and I didn't want him to.

Rita Rudner

Marriage and Divorce

Men who have pierced ears are better prepared for marriage.
They've experienced pain and bought jewellery.

Rita Rudner

When you see what some girls marry, you realize how they
must hate to work for a living.

Helen Rowland

I consider everybody as having a right to marry once in their
lives for Love, if they can.

Jane Austen

When a girl marries a man she is sadly aware that all his old
sweethearts are wondering how she did it, and that all her
old sweethearts are wondering why.

Helen Rowland

I never married because there was no need. I have three pets
at home which answer the same purpose as a husband. I have
a dog which growls every morning, a parrot which swears all
afternoon, and a cat that comes home late at night.

Marie Corelli

Verily, verily, an husband is a work of art which must be
executed by hand; for there is no factory which turneth
them out to order.

Helen Rowland

A man in love is incomplete until he has married. Then he's
finished.

Zsa Zsa Gabor

Marriage and Divorce

I married beneath me, all women do.

Nancy Astor

Bigamy is having one husband too many. Monogamy is the same.

Anonymous

I loathe the very principle of matrimony. It must end in failure, & it is death to a woman's personality. She must drop the theme & begin to start playing the accompaniment. For me there is no attraction.

Katherine Mansfield

He would have to marry some day, he knew. It was an obligation laid upon him together with the family seat and comfortable income to which he had succeeded before his two-and-twentieth birthday. The thing would have to be done — but he meant to delay the evil hour as long as he could, and to be monstrously exacting as to the fairy princess for whose dear sake he should put on those domestic fetters.

Mary Braddon

I knew that the men I married were very attractive to the opposite sex: the twenty marriages they had between them proves that, if nothing else does.

Ava Gardner

At twenty-five she had married Howard Talbot — for love? — no, not exactly, for a much more usual reason — propinquity — the same set at Newport, and Sadie Dent have desired him.

Elinor Glyn, describing Bella Van Demen

Even when a man knows that he wants to marry a woman, she has to prove it to him with a diagram before he is really convinced of it.

Helen Rowland

Why do men marry? Always to secure something.

Elinor Glyn

The man who chose his wife to match his drawing-room curtains was a man of taste.

Mrs Fanny Douglas

I'd rather be flayed alive! Ugh! married to Hugh! I should be dead of disgust in a week! Faugh!

Rhoda Broughton

Indeed he has all the qualities that would make a husband tolerable — battlement, veranda, stable, etc., no grins and no glass in his eye.

George Eliot

The only really happy people are married women and single men.

Marlene Dietrich

One wishes marriage for one's daughter and, for one's descendants, better luck.

Rita Rudner

Marriage and Divorce

Whenever I date a guy I think, is this the man I want my children to spend their weekends with?

Rita Rudner

Now I'm free! And the man who caused me so much pain now says, "I want to marry you". And I say, "Who doesn't?"

Oprah Winfrey

Marriage, as our world sees it, is simply a convenience; a somewhat clumsy contrivance to tide over a social difficulty.

Ouida

Marriage seems to be as general this year as influenza.

Elizabeth Carter

Why on earth should I be foolish enough to marry?

Rachel Félix

What else was marriage but support in return for sexual service and cohabitation.

Germaine Greer

I was a lawyer for twenty years. I think like a lawyer. That is not often the best thing for somebody in my position.

Hillary Rodham Clinton

I didn't want five husbands, but it happened that way and that's all there is to it.

Rita Hayworth

Marry rich. Buy him a pacemaker, then stand behind him and say "boo".

Joan Rivers

Women are putting off marriage for as long as they can — because every wedding has to have a bridegroom.

Julie Burchill

The Hen Night should be held sufficiently in advance of the wedding to allow for complete recovery following a liver transplant.

Jenny Eclair

Queen Victoria didn't like weddings, considering that they had an indelicate flavour. I think she was right.

Alice Thomas Ellis

Liz Taylor likes getting married. I like being married. There's a difference.

Mitzi Gaynor

Goodwill and desire are perhaps, peculiarly and sadly, twins that sit incompatibly in the domestic nest.

Naomi Segal

Wonder if Adam ever scolded Eve for her extravagance in fig leaves.

Helen Rowland

Aging millionaires who marry twenty-five-year-old part-owners of mobile homes in search of rejuvenation don't get rejuvenated. They get worn out.

Germaine Greer

Have you noticed that all the husbands like her? All, I mean, except her own?

Edith Wharton

It is against the best interests of social intercourse to invite husbands and wives to the same party. Besides cramping each other's exaggerations, they are given to cross-talking.

Lillian Day

These days if your skin's cleared up you're too old to marry … Men are walking down the aisle with a foetus in a veil.

Kathy Lette

On my own account, I have indulged in a matrimonial scheme, but the gentleman is so dreadfully in love with himself that I have not patience, energy, hope, or inclination enough to persevere.

Geraldine Endsor Jewsbury

I'd be frantic did I have to face the same man over the table every morning. Besides, I always eat breakfast in bed. Aggressive males get up and thresh about and snort under the shower.

Tallulah Bankhead

Marriage and Divorce

There is nothing like a man for trying the temper. Mark my word, it is because there is no marrying or giving in marriage in heaven that the temper of an angel is the temper of an angel. If the angels had got husbands, there'd be a different tale about their tempers.

Ellen T. Fowler

A man without a wife is as a helpless barge without a tow-boat.

Helen Rowland

You never hear of an unhappy marriage unless the neighbours have heard it first.

Lillian Russell

There are two kinds of people you cannot buy presents for. One is men; the other is husbands. If your husband is a man, the situation is utterly impossible.

Alice Kahn

There is no such thing as a good husband or a sweet onion.

Rumanian proverb

No man can sit down and love a woman eighteen hours a day, not actively.

Charlotte Perkins Gilman

I could never be lonely without a husband.

Lillian Russell

Marriage and Divorce

There are thousands of homes where unhappiness reigns, where joy might have lived, but for the grudging of agreeable words on the part of the husband.

Elinor Glyn

Real husbands, like real terrapins, once so plentiful in this country that even the poor could afford to indulge in them every day, have now become so scarce that they are a luxury of the rich.

Dorothy Dix

Every time I see a headline about wife-swapping I read on eagerly; but it always turns out to be swapping just for the night. And where's the percentage in that?

Katharine Whitehorn

Married men have a habit of making even the most confident woman turn into something of a walking cliché.

Paula Yates

To me marriage is for five or ten years.

Cher

Carl would rather have his body hair painfully pulled out than spend money. I call him Scrooge. He's so tight he squeaks when he walks.

Dolly Parton on her husband, Carl Dean

The wrong people always have nice things — even husbands!

Norma Lorimer

I no longer dine in private houses, I can't stand the repressed sex and overt violence.

Sue Townsend

I've married a few people I shouldn't have, but haven't we all?

Mamie Van Doren

The medical term for a woman paralysed from the waist down and the neck up is "marriage".

Kathy Lette

A woman's husband of course must keep her. It's his right. What did he marry for?

Augusta Johnstone

In his soul every husband feels that he has conferred such an inestimable boon upon his wife by marrying her that she can never really repay him, anyway, but that it is up to her to keep busy on the job.

Dorothy Dix

You will, of course, lose all your friends when you marry.

Elizabeth Hawes

The guy who used to appear at your front door every night because he was wild to see you, now appears there every night because that's where he happens to live.

Lucille Kallen

The amount of bile that he brings home is awfully grand.
Jane Carlyle on her husband, Thomas

NEGATIVE KINDNESS. — Do the doctors know that half
the wives in the world die of this complaint? "He never
spoke an unkind word to his wife." Yes; but did he
remember, now and then, to speak a kind one?
Fanny Fern

Our marriage licence turned out to be a learner's permit.
Joan Rivers

Who are you? Who needs you? You're just the lady who does
the washing and ironing and cooking and cleaning and
yelling.
Lucille Kallen

I defy you to put any blissfully happy married couple under
a blanket with a single control and have them speaking to
one another in the cold light of morning.
Erma Bombeck

Wives are like cockroaches. Also part of a great historical
tradition. They will survive you after a nuclear attack.
Lorrie Moore

I have learned there is little difference in husbands. You
might as well keep the first.
Adela Rogers St John

He believed that all women who want to should be free, equal, independent, creative, well-informed, and lead stimulating, interesting lives. Except me.

Lucille Kallen

Before marriage, a man will lie awake all night thinking about something you said; after marriage, he'll fall asleep before you finish saying it.

Helen Rowland

Love is a farce; matrimony is a humbug; husbands are domestic Napoleons, Neroes, Alexanders — sighing for other hearts to conquer, after they are sure of yours.

Fanny Fern

A good wife is always her husband's "guide, philosopher and friend"; also his guardian, digestion, conscience, time-table and valet.

Helen Rowland

Though courtship turns frogs into princes, marriage turns them quietly back.

Marge Piercy

Husband and wife gazed steadily at each other without a word. No word was needed, for in that look there passed, like a sword-thrust, the vision of an eternal rancour.

Ella Hepworth Dixon

If you cannot have your dear husband for a comfort and a delight, for a breadwinner and a crosspatch, for a sofa, chair, or hot water bottle, one can use him as a Cross to be borne.

Stevie Smith

Smile! It flatters your husband. He wants to be considered the source of your happiness; whether he was baptized Nero or Moses! ... Besides, you miserable little whimperer, what have you to cry for? A-i-n-t y-o-u m-a-r-r-i-e-d? Isn't that the summum bonum — the height of feminine ambition? ...You've nothing to do but retire on your laurels, and spend the rest of your life endeavouring to be thankful that you are Mrs John Smith! "Smile!" you simpleton!

Fanny Fern

A woman may owe a man a lovin', but not a livin' ...

Mae West

She had given her life into his keeping, and he had put it away like a garment, neatly cleaned and ironed and never to be worn.

Alice Thomas Ellis

Every time he got on a plane, I would imagine the plane crash, and the funeral ... and flirting at the funeral, and how soon I could start dating after the funeral.

Nora Ephron

Wonder how many wives have been awakened from love's young dream by a snore.

Helen Rowland

Marriage and Divorce

A husband is a convenient part of the furniture of a house, unless he be a clumsy fixture.

Mary Wollstonecraft

In the bloom of his youth, impatient for wealth and ambitious of power, he had tied himself to a rich dowager of quality, whose age, though sixty-seven, was but among the smaller species of her evil properties, her disposition being far more repulsive than her wrinkles.

Fanny Burney

My husband is certainly not amiable.

George Sand

"Which are you, in love or out of love with Mr Selwyn?" — "Neither, my child, neither. He never molests me, never intrudes his dear dull personage on my society."

Lady Caroline Lamb on her husband

The honeymoon is as short-lived as a lucifer-match; after that you may wear your wedding-dress at the wash tub, and your night-cap to a meeting, and your husband wouldn't know it.

Fanny Fern

Happiness in marriage is entirely a matter of chance.

Jane Austen

When two people marry they become in the eyes of the law one person, and that one person is the husband.

Shana Alexander

Marriage and Divorce

A wife is only pleasant when her husband is out of the way.
She must either be in love, or out of love with him. If the
latter, they wrangle; and if the former, it is ten times worse.
Lovers are at all times insufferable; but when the holy laws of
matrimony give them a lawful right to be so amazingly fond
and affectionate, it makes one sick.

Lady Caroline Lamb

No woman with brains hath ever plucked a peach in the
Garden of Matrimony. Nay, it is not given unto one woman
to possess both real ability and a real husband.

Helen Rowland

Haven't you ever thought long and hard about that man,
your husband? Don't answer me wittily and evasively:"Yes,
since I started cheating on him!"

Colette

"How I do dislike my husband," a young married peeress,
who had better be nameless, said to Addle at a dinner party
shortly before the war. My husband, unable to believe his
ears, thought she must be talking of dustbins and replied:
"Smelly things, I believe."

Mary Dunn

Marriage gave me the courage to go into showbusiness.

Joan Rivers

An archaeologist is the best husband any woman can have:
the older she gets, the more interested he is in her.

Agatha Christie

Marriage and Divorce

I had no wish for a second husband. I had enough of the first. I like to have my own way — to lie down mistress, and get up master.

Susanna Moodie

Alma: I rather suspect her of being in love with him.
Martin: Her own husband? Monstrous! What a selfish woman!

Jennie Jerome Churchill

A husband is what is left of the lover after the nerve has been extracted.

Helen Rowland

It should be a very happy marriage — they are both so much in love with him.

Irene Thomas

I am a source of satisfaction to him, a nurse, a piece of furniture, a woman — nothing more.

Sophie Tolstoy

Margot is a good wife; she allows her husband to sap her energy and youth, and tax her good nature, and feels no resentment.

Fay Weldon

Personally, I know nothing about sex because I've always been married.

Zsa Zsa Gabor

Marriage and Divorce

My mother said it was simple to keep a man, you must be a maid in the living room, a cook in the kitchen and a whore in the bedroom. I said I'd hire the other two and take care of the bedroom bit.

Jerry Hall

The reason that husbands and wives do not understand each other is because they belong to different sexes.

Dorothy Dix

Good marriages are seldom celebrated, while every tiff or spat in a celebrity marriage becomes tabloid fodder.

Hillary Rodham Clinton

After a few years of marriage a man can look right at a woman without seeing her and a woman can see right through a man without looking at him.

Helen Rowland

But sexual politics in the workplace is easy compared to the sexual politics in your own kitchen.

Vicki Woods

The graveyards are full of women whose houses were so spotless you could eat off the floor. Remember the second wife always has a maid.

Heloise Cruse

I gave up dreaming years ago. All I do now is cook and scrub and change my library book.

Sue Arnold

Home is the girl's prison and the woman's workhouse.

Florence Farr

I've always believed that the concept of the Jewish princess was invented by a Jewish prince who couldn't get his wife to fetch him the butter.

Nora Ephron

The permanent error of the housewife lies in the assumption that her love for her family makes her service satisfactory.

Charlotte Perkins

If the truth be told, most housework can be omitted without grave consequences.

Lucy Ellmann

Yes, I hate hate HATE doing these things that you accept just as all men accept of their women ... I detest this woman who "superintends" you and rushes about, slamming doors & slopping water — all untidy with her blouse out & her nails grimed. I am disgusted & repelled by the creature who shouts at you "you might at least empty the pail & wash out the tea leaves!"

Katherine Mansfield

DIVORCE

Now my acquaintance is divided fairly evenly between those who are desperate to get married and those who are equally desperate to get divorced.

Alice Thomas Ellis

Marriage and Divorce

I am nearly as keen on divorce as I am on shopping.

India Knight

Divorce is the sacrament of adultery.

Sophie Arnould

There are men I could spend eternity with, but not this life.

Kathleen Norris

I'd marry again if I found a man who had $15 million and would sign over half of it to me before the marriage, and guarantee he'd be dead within a year.

Bette Davis

Marriage is a great institution, but I'm not ready for an institution.

Mae West

Sure I want a man in my life, but not in my house. I want him to hook up the VCR and leave. Why should I want him in the house?

Joy Behar

If divorce has increased one thousand per cent, don't blame the woman's movement. Blame our obsolete sex roles on which our marriages were based.

Betty Friedan

Marriage and Divorce

I only knew one thing for sure. Marriage was definitely the chief cause of divorce.

Kathy Lette

Husbands are like fires. They go out when unattended.

Zsa Zsa Gabor

So that ends my first experience with matrimony, which I always thought a highly overrated performance.

Isadora Duncan

In losing a husband one loses a master who is often an obstacle to the enjoyment of many things.

Madeleine de Scudéry

Better to have loved and lost than to have spent your whole damn life with him.

Graffiti

Get a job, your husband hates you. Get a good job, your husband leaves you. Get a stupendous job, your husband leaves you for a teenager.

Cynthia Heimel

Divorce may be the only human disaster that translates into money and well as giggles ... The survivors of these battles are hors de combat — or is it whores de combat?

Rita Mae Brown

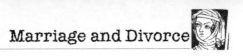

A bride at her second wedding does not wear a veil. She wants to see what she is getting.

Helen Rowland

I've always been amused when people mix me up with Edna Wallace Hopper. Sure we share the same last name, but the wrong number. She was three; I was number five, as in Chanel.

Hedda Hopper, on her husband's third wife.

Changing husbands is about as satisfactory as changing a bundle from one hand to the other; it gives you only temporary relief.

Helen Rowland

Modesty forbids that I mention the lawyers — just in case children should pick up this book.

Rita Mae Brown

Never give back the ring. Never. Swallow it first.

Joan Rivers

The wages of sin is alimony.

Carolyn Wells

Happy Families

Happy Families

Home is definitely where the heartache is.

Kathy Lette

The way to cure homesickness is to go home.

Edna Ferber

The sanctity of the home is another dominant myth.

Charlotte Perkins Gilman

Home is the cornerstone of American Life. Living in it is a pain in the neck.

Elizabeth Hawes

Families are the main source of guilt and therefore must be got rid of, either by suffocation or alienation.

Jenny Eclair

All my family have inherited histrionic ability to a marked degree.

Mary Dunn

Two women a week are currently being murdered by the man they live with and one child a week by its father or stepfather — but hey, the family that slays together stays together!

Julie Burchill

Tell the truth and shame the family.

Ethel Watts Mumford

You hear a lot of dialogue on the death of the American family. Families aren't dying. They're merging into big conglomerates.

Erma Bombeck

But of all the small sufferings of existence there are few more trying than a continual sense, or dread, of being "rubbed up the wrong way" by somebody whom you are bound to love.

Dinah Craik

Often the reason we cannot get along with our own families is because they are like a mirror in which we see our own faults in all their hideousness.

Dorothy Dix

My family were of good English peasant class from St John's Wood.

Hermione Gingold

Aristo-prats always use the fact that their parents didn't love them to go round causing havoc. No wonder their parents didn't love them, the nasty little gutless inbreds.

Jenny Eclair

All I heard when I was growing up was "Why can't you be more like your cousin Sheila? Why can't you be more like your cousin Sheila?"
Sheila died at birth.

Joan Rivers

Happy Families

I hated rows unless I made them myself.

Gertrude Atherton

Being a mother is a noble status, right? Right. So why does it change when you put "unwed" or "welfare" in front of it?

Florynce R. Kennedy

The mother or mistress of a large family is in the case of a tethered nag, always treading and subsisting on the same spot.

Hester Thrale

There's some sort of mother blood that just wants you to buy firearms when you have a child.

Courtney Love

Can I tell you how much I loved my mother? I loved her like a dog loves an old bone.

Julia Darling

Mother is the dead heart of the family, spending father's earnings on consumer goods to enhance the environment in which he eats, sleeps and watches the television.

Germaine Greer

I think it's a mother's duty to embarrass their children.

Cher

Happy Families

I've always blamed my shortcomings as a mother on the fact that I studied Child Psychology and Discipline under an unmarried professor whose only experience was in raising a dog.

Erma Bombeck

It takes a woman twenty years to make a man of her son, and another woman twenty minutes to make a fool of him.

Helen Rowland

Babies need mothers. Sometimes lawyers, housewives, pilots, writers and electricians also need mothers.

Judith Viorst

Maureen was an only child. Maureen's mother having scorned her father right out of the house, shortly after Maureen's birth.

Fay Weldon

I decided that Whistler's Mother was going to seem like Medea when compared to the perfection of my motherhood.

Helen Hayes

Give a child what it wants and it's gone for ever.

Fay Weldon

No man is responsible for his father. That is entirely his mother's affair.

Margaret Turnbull

Happy Families

Even though all fathers are physically exhausted and mentally denuded, they like to talk. Encourage Dad to talk. Probably no one has for years.

Elizabeth Hawes

Mrs Turner and her nine daughters! It is a public calamity, Mrs Turner being so very prolific — the produce so frightful. Amongst other animals, when they commit such blunders, the brood is drowned.

Lady Caroline Lamb

If Everybody Else's Mother turned up at a PTA meeting and identified herself, she would be lynched.

Erma Bombeck

If we had not been pretty, I think we would have been drowned like little dogs. That's my mother!

Zsa Zsa Gabor on her mother, Jolie

Milady had two leading characteristics — a major one and a minor one. The major one was an ineradicable conviction that no young woman and few mature ones could look upon her son without "lusting after him", to lead him to the altar — a position which demanded the most sleepless vigilance on her part.

Rhoda Broughton

Grannies are only cute on TV. In real life they're like Oxfam shops on legs.

Pamela Stephenson

GIVING BIRTH

They say men can never experience the pain of childbirth ... they can if you hit them in the goolies with a cricket bat ... for fourteen hours.

Jo Brand

Mrs Hall of Sherbourn was brought to bed yesterday of a dead child, some weeks before she expected, owing to a fright. — I suppose she happened unawares to look at her husband.

Jane Austen

I realize why women die in childbirth — it's preferable.

Sherry Glaser

Of course, the placenta is very useful because it is so very hideous that by comparison, the baby is quite attractive.

Jenny Eclair

To simulate the birth experience, take one car jack, insert into rectum, pump to maximum height and replace with jack hammer. And that would be a good birth.

Kathy Lette

When he called the hospital to report that I was in labour, the nurse, trying to calm Fang down, said: "Is this her first baby?" He said: "No, this is her husband."

Phyllis Diller

There were twins in the first year! that was humiliating enough! So bourgeois! — Twins! Fat, slobbering creatures with a strong look of the Buggins family.

Elinor Glyn

I think I must have been elected chairman of the entertainment committee at birth. My mother confessed that she had to smile when she first saw me.

Marie Dressler

The Solomons, male and female, have puzzled their heads in vain to find an acceptable plaything for a baby ... Baby hates the beaten track.

Fanny Fern

CHILDREN/CHILDHOOD

At the moment one's children are conceived, one ceases to be an ego and becomes merely a cosmic tube, a funnel into timelessness.

Erica Jong

Do you wonder why the Tooth Fairy continues to be the only growth industry in Britain? Fifty pence a tooth and double if you forget to let her in.

Maureen Lipman

There's no sense in pretending that grown-up sons and daughters are still babies and that they need you. They don't. Let them do their own sinking or swimming while you indulge in a little fancy diving.

Marie Dressler

Children should realize that parents are emotionally insecure.

Jean Kerr

I don't care if people think I'm exploiting my child. She's the only successful thing I've done in my life.

Courtney Love

I was brought up differently from the average American, because the average child is brought up expecting to be happy.

Marilyn Monroe

There are other weapons in the child-rearing armoury besides battleaxes. Bribery, for instance, and blackmail.

Sue Arnold

All of us have to recognize that we owe our children more than we have been giving them.

Hillary Rodham Clinton

The children never forgave me. Oedipus only killed his father and married his mother, but I sold their Nintendo.

Sue Arnold

My folks? That's just it. If the Prodigal Son had been a daughter they'd probably have handed her one of her sister's mother hubbards, and put her to work washing dishes in the kitchen.

Edna Ferber

It's never too late for a happy childhood.

Gloria Steinem

No one has a normal childhood.

Laura Chester

Children should be judged on what they are — a punishment for an early marriage.

Erma Bombeck

We have made mistakes with our children, which will undoubtedly become clearer as they get old enough to write their own books.

Jean Kerr

Having children accentuates more marital faults than adultery does.

Julie Burchill

One of the reasons children are such duds socially is that they say things like "When do you think you're going to be dead, Grandma?"

Jean Kerr

Upper-middle-class men believe in discipline to the extent that they beat their children with wooden spoons and then get all confused when they get an erection.

Jenny Eclair

Happy Families

The great thing is not to expect too much from children. You know the quotation, "Blessed is he who expecteth nothing".

Diana Woods

I am going to tell you about my children. Before they tell you about me.

Maureen Lipman

I think children shouldn't be seen or heard.

Jo Brand

An Infant Prodigy is nothing more than a rug-rat with unbelievably ambitious parents.

Kathy Lette

Even when freshly washed and relieved of all obvious confections, children tend to be sticky. One can only assume this has something to do with not smoking enough.

Fran Lebowitz

When the history of guilt is written, parents who refuse their children money will be right up there in the Top Ten.

Erma Bombeck

Childhood is a swindle, a very unequal bargain.

Lucy Ellmann

Happy Families

SIBLINGS

Brothers and sisters are put on this earth to be teased and made to cry.

Jenny Eclair

I suppose it was good that my brothers fought each other. As it turned out, they would need the practice.

Dolly Parton

I have got a little brother two years old. I am eight. He always cries when you stick pins in him.

Unknown

A friend: I don't know why Connie works so hard. After all she can't take it with her.
Bennett's sister: If Connie can't take it with her, she won't go.

Exchange on Constance Bennett

Of course, I could always depend on my brothers to tell me how bad I looked.

Dolly Parton

I know that small children have a certain animal magnetism. People kiss them a lot. But are they really in demand, socially?

Jean Kerr

You will say that Esther was not alone, that she had her brother to look at [the moon] with her; but who will deny that a brother who makes agricultural remarks about the Queen of the Night, and observes that the haze around her royal head looks well for the turnips, is worse, immeasurably worse, than nobody?

Rhoda Broughton

Who Needs
Enemies?

Familiarity doesn't breed contempt; it is contempt.

Florence King

A new acquaintance is like a new novel; you open it with expectation, but what you find there seldom makes you care to take it off the shelf another time.

Ouida

One seeks new friends only when too well known by old ones.

Madame de Puisieux

To keep all your old friends is like keeping all your old clothes.

Helen Gurley Brown

Sometimes you have a friend and you think they are made of rock, and suddenly you realize they're only made of sand.

Maria Callas

I have my bitchy side, but I don't think I'm really nasty. I think that a lot of other people probably think that I am. Fuck them.

Debbie Harry

Newish friends, if they get ghastly, can be weighed and found wanting, but you'd never do a thing like that to old ones; their terrible habits are just part of the universe.

Katharine Whitehorn

Neighbours. I'd rather have thrush.

Pamela Stephenson

I do not want people to be very agreeable, as it saves me the trouble of liking them a great deal.

Jane Austen

If you write to someone twice a week there is much to tell; twice a year and there is hardly a thing.

Peg Bracken

Many years ago we knew a girl who called herself a friend. She was so sweet that if you bit her you'd damage your teeth.

Alice Thomas Ellis

Always be nice to other girls. If you don't, they will find some underhand way of getting even with you.

Elizabeth Hawes

Many sarcastic and true words have been said by man, and in no jealous spirit, concerning woman's friendship for woman. The passing judgement of the majority of men on such devotion might be summed up in the words, "Occupy till I come". It does occupy till they come. And if they don't come, the hastily improvised friendship may hold together for years, like an unseaworthy boat in a harbour, which looks like a boat, but never goes out to sea.

Mary Cholmondeley

Great friendships are never at ease.

Marie de Sévigné

The inert force of the deep-settled love she bore herself was wonderful.

Charlotte Brontë

No insect hangs its nest on threads as frail as those which will sustain the weight of human vanity.

Edith Wharton

It is less mortifying to believe one's self unpopular than insignificant, and vanity prefers to assume that indifference is a latent form of unfriendliness.

Edith Wharton

GOSSIP

Last night I dined out in Chelsea, and mauled the dead and rotten carcases of several works written by my friends.

Virginia Woolf

Come to me in your joys, my dear, and come to me in your sorrows, but not in between whiles. I've no time for chit-chat.

Lilian Baylis

Even the discreetest friends will, like the closest-packed hold of a ship, leak occasionally. Salt water and secrets are alike apt to ooze.

Ouida

He's the kind of man who picks his friends — to pieces.

Mae West

A little Scandal now and then with a Female Neighbour will add to the Charms of rustic life.

Hester Thrale

Silent women are seldom bores — it is the talkative ones who make one feel limp!

Elinor Glyn

If you can't say anything good about someone, sit right here by me.

Alice Roosevelt Longsworth

Never trust a man with another's secret, never trust a woman with her own.

Lady Elizabeth Melbourne

SPECIFIC FRIENDS

We have just got to know a wonderful Lady Ottoline Morrell, who has the head of a Medusa; but she is very simple and innocent in spite of it, and worships the arts.

Virginia Woolf

Virginia Woolf … wouldn't be good in a crowd.

Lady Ottoline Morrell

His odd propensity to vomit his friends after a certain period has to be taken into account in his psychological portraits.
Lady Ottoline Morrell on D. H. Lawrence

"I hear," said Miss Crisp next morning, addressing Susannah Henley, "that you told Parthenope I was a spiteful old toad."
Rhoda Broughton

Topaz was wonderfully patient — but I sometimes wonder if it is not only patience, but also a faint resemblance to cows.
Dodie Smith

Miss Fletcher and I were very thick, but I am the thinnest of the two — She wore her purple Muslin, which is pretty enough, tho' it does not become her complexion. There are two Traits in her Character which are pleasing; namely, she admires Camilla, & drinks no cream in her Tea.
Jane Austen

That woman is a real Devil — I could no more endure her than the perpetual sight of a dozen crawling toads.
Mary Shelley

"He would not touch Amaryllis with a pair of tongs," cry I.
Rhoda Broughton

The affair between Margot Asquith and Margot Asquith will live as one of the prettiest love stories in all literature.
Dorothy Parker

She really is very close to a charming character; if she had had the small pox she would have been so.

> *Mrs Gaskell on Effie Gray, John Ruskin's wife*

Watching Tallulah on stage is like watching somebody skating on thin ice. Everyone wants to be there when it breaks.

> *Mrs Patrick Campbell, referring to Tallulah Bankhead*

We continue to see one another like two people that are resolved to hate with civility.

> *Lady Mary Wortley Montagu on her relationship with the Duchess of Marlborough*

To hear Alice talk about her escape from France, one would have thought she had swum the Channel with her maid between her teeth.

> *Mrs Ronald Greville, referring to Alice Keppel, Edward VII's mistress*

It certainly is not pleasant to hear of God and Miss Biddeford in a breath. Still some sparkles show where gems might in better days be more easily disengaged from the rubbish. She is still valuable as a disturbing force to the lazy.

> *Margaret Fuller*

I like Lady H. too well not to wish that she had never learned to sing, for certainly her talents do not lie that way.

> *Lady Palmerston, writing about Lady Emma Hamilton, Nelson's mistress*

I cannot compassionate the countess, since I think her
insolent character deserves all the mortifications Heaven can
send her.

Lady Mary Wortley Montagu

There are three teachers in the school ... The two first have
no particular character. One is an old maid, and the other
will be one.

Charlotte Brontë

I can't tell whether you know a tall, musical, silly, ugly thing,
niece to Lady Essex Roberts, who is called Miss Legh.

Lady Mary Wortley Montagu

Everina was never a favourite with any one — & now she is
the most intolerable of God's creatures. The worst is, that
being poor & friendless, it is on my conscience to pay her
attention — and she is so disagreeable to me, that I know no
punishment so great as spending an hour in her Company.

Mary Shelley on her aunt Everina

"Dear Miss Green! Oh, she would not mind, She is so
pleased with her own conversation that it does not matter
whether people listen or not. She is a lady who shakes hands
with herself every morning and says, 'My dear soul, you are
really the cleverest, wittiest, brightest creature I know — not
exactly beautiful, but infinitely charming,' and in that
humour she comes smiling down to breakfast, and lets us all
see what poor creatures she thinks us."

Mary Braddon

Bimbos, Himbos & Bluestockings

BLUESTOCKINGS & BIMBOS

All the brains the bluestockings will ever pile up will not be worth one complexion.

Gertrude Atherton

You see these gray hairs? Well, making whoopee with the intelligentsia was the way I earned them.

Dorothy Parker

In general, and almost universally, the feminine intellect has less strength but more acuteness.

Laetitia Matilda Hawkins

You may at times have the sensation you are being written down to. This is because your Beauty Quotient is supposed to be twice your Intelligence Quotient.

Elizabeth Hawes

There is a personality lamp behind your eyes. Make sure that your personality current is on. Sometimes it is necessary to connect the switch and make it function.

Renee Long

It is a common failing of an ambitious mind to overrate itself.

Lady Caroline Lamb

True philosophy raises us above grandeur, but nothing can raise us above the ennui which it causes.

Madame de Maintenon

Nothing is so pleasant as to display your worldly wisdom in epigram and dissertation, but it is a trifle tedious to hear another person display theirs.

Ouida

The best kissers are often nearly illiterate.

India Knight

Me, I never saw a definition of happiness that could detain me after train-time.

Dorothy Parker

Fools love folly, and wise men wisdom.

Marguerite de Valois

Generally speaking, it is inhumane to detain a fleeting insight.

Fran Lebowitz

Truisms are also true.

Gloria Steinem

There was nothing wrong with her that a vasectomy of the vocal chords wouldn't fix.

Lisa Alther

She'd never make the same mistake again:
She always made a new mistake instead.

Wendy Cope

If I meet people who are dense enough to take my innocent fantasies for hypocritical vices I cannot persuade myself to take the trouble to undeceive them.

George Sand

We must love stupid people better than ourselves; are they not the really unfortunate ones of this world? Do not people without taste and without ideal grow constantly weary, rejoicing in nothing, and being quite useless here below?

George Sand

Brains are a handicap for a blonde.

Paula Yates

You can lead a horticulture, but you can't make her think.

Dorothy Parker

It cannot, I think, be truly asserted, that the intellectual powers know no difference of sex. Nature certainly intended a distinction; but it is a distinction which is far from degrading us.

Laetitia Matilda Hawkins

In my day, women were still stud beasts, and feminine wit wasn't fashionable. It was a privilege reserved exclusively to the men.

Rachel Ferguson

Any woman who lets a man walk over her is a dumb idiot and deserves no better.

Edith Piaf

It is remarkable how little some men can be, how childish, although adorned with hirsute appendages and looking, as far as the outer man goes, intelligent. Yet their talk is all lisped nothings.

Anonymous 19th-century writer

Gentlemen: when you "come down" to commonplace or small-talk with an intelligent lady, one of two things is the consequence: she either recognizes the condescension and despises you, or else she accepts it as the highest intellectual effort of which you are capable, and rates you accordingly.

Mrs E. B. Duffey

In general all curvaceousness strikes men as incompatible with the life of the mind.

Françoise Parturier

The great and almost only comfort about being a woman is that one can always pretend to be more stupid than one is, and no one is surprised.

Freya Stark

They thought that being impervious to algebra I'd be impervious to anything, even contamination and propinquity.

May Vokes

Daisy graduated also. It was common knowledge that she passed English because Mr Davidson craved her every inch.

Jane Hamilton

Bimbos...

I went to a girls' school and it made me so stupid that I could barely remember how to breathe.

India Knight

Millionaires and jet-set studs will only tolerate stupidity in very young women.

Germaine Greer

I don't suppose anyone who knows me gives me much credit for being a brainy dame.

Rita Hayworth

She thinks Bosnia Herzegovina's the Wonderbra model.

Isabel Wolff

Oh dear, why does Lydia always come in — and why must she beg me to believe that she thinks seriously every day of her life, as she says? When her brain is a cage of canaries?

Virginia Woolf, referring to the Russian ballerina Lydia Lopokova

Dietrich? That contraption! She was one of the beautiful-but-dumb girls, like me, but she belonged to the category of those who thought they were smart and fooled other people into believing it.

Louise Brooks on Marlene Dietrich

She is a little coxcombical and affects to be learned.

Mrs Delaney

The basis of Colette's unique power as a novelist was that she wrote straight from the emotions; nothing mental ever got in her way.

Anita Loos

Clara was the idol of the illiterate, and from her dainty lips came nothing more seductive than bubble gum.

Anita Loos on Clara Bow

Who does not feel sympathy for Susan Anthony? She has striven long and earnestly to become a man ... She has never done any good in the world, but then she doesn't think so.

Ida Husted Harper

Mrs Green found great delight in ringing bells, and giving orders. Women who have sprung from nothing frequently do.

Lady Wasteneys

And yes, making Posh Spice look dumb didn't turn out to be all that hard.

Zoe Williams

She was born with a birch-broom in her hand, and worst of all was a shameless flatterer and insatiable of flattery.

Caroline Bowles on English reformer Hannah More

There goes a woman who knows all the things that can be taught and none of the things that cannot be taught.

Coco Chanel

Bimbos...

A little upstart, vulgar being, with her Mr E. and her *caro sposo*, and her resources, and all her air of pert pretension and underbred finery.

Jane Austen

She is completely without originality. Everybody is unable to understand her and thinks that this is because she is too original or is trying too hard to be original. But she is only divinely inspired in ordinariness.

Laura Riding on Gertrude Stein

Ava knew as much of life and the ways of humans as it is possible to know by skirting actual experience.

Elinor Glyn on Ava Cleveland

Rose Macaulay is bored. Her writing is emancipatedly spinsterish.

Elizabeth Hawes

The Brontës would have excited an investigating psychiatrist. They were neurotic. But they did not know that. They took themselves to be geniuses.

Margaret Lawrence

Hannah More did get unendurably poky, narrow, and solemn in her last days ... we naturally think of her as an aged spinster with black mitts, corkscrew curls and a mob cap.

Kate Sanborn

The most thorough emetic I know of, is in the shape of Guide to Young Wives, and kindred books.

Fanny Fern

So dumb that I can't tell a hardy annual from an effete perennial, and I've always thought convolvulus was something you sent for the doctor to stop. I guess I'm not sufficiently horticultured.

Cornelia Otis Skinner

The Boston woman draweth down her mouth, rolleth up her eyes, foldeth her hands, and walketh on a crack. She rejoiceth in anatomical and chemical lectures. She prateth of Macauley and Carlyle; belongeth to many and divers reading-classes, and smileth in a chaste, moonlight kind of way on literary men.

Fanny Fern

I've been called many things, but never an intellectual.

Tallulah Bankhead

I spent the morning with the Young-and-Pretty-Married-Woman, with a skin-like-a-magnolia-flower-and-ah-such-an-arrogant-mouse! So if this letter should prove dull, well, you will understand why; for she has sucked my brains as your grandmother was taught to suck eggs.

Edith Sitwell

Do you know that Mme B. is writing a fiction — and would have it believed that your friend — and then Trelawny and then everyone have been in love with her — ...Ah! yes in love — as rabbits are of hunters; She giving them chase — but could never run fast enough to catch up with them; they all would escape her.

Mary Shelley

Bimbos ...

I have got several very bad new lunatics, most of them religious, and some "just ordinary housewives, who try to write a little".

Edith Sitwell, referring to guests at a forthcoming party at her house

Madame M. [Merveilleux du Platis] might go on exceedingly well & gain if she had the brains of a goose but her head is a sive [sic] & her temper worse than wildfire it is gunpowder and blows up everything.

Mary Shelley

I cannot call you a goose — as the geese saved the capitol, and no amount of your imbecile cackling would awaken anybody. I cannot call you an ass, as Balaam's constant companion saw and recognized an angel. I can only gather, therefore, that you are one of the vegetable kingdom and that all this sizzling and squeaking of yours is due to the decaying of a vegetable.

Edith Sitwell to an unnamed female American gossip writer

She was merely distinguishable from nothing by her simple good nature, the inextricable entanglement of her thoughts, her love of letter writing, and her friendship with Lady Maclaughlan.

Susan Ferrier

I wonder by what accident Miss Seward came by her fame. Setting aside her pedantry and presumption, there is no poet male or female who ever clothed so few ideas in so many words. She is all tinkling and tinsel — a sort of Dr Darwin in petticoats.

Mary Russell Mitford

Miss Jacky, the senior of the trio, was what is reckoned a very sensible woman — which generally means, a very disagreeable, obstinate, illiberal director of all men, women, and children — a sort of superintendent of all actions, time, and place — with unquestioned authority to arraign, judge, and condemn, upon the statutes of her own supposed sense.

Susan Ferrier

Lady Portmore had talked unceasingly for an hour and a half; and though from the vague diffusiveness of her words, and the hopeless entanglement of her ideas, it was difficult to ascertain the precise purport of her remarks, Helen felt that the general result was irritating.

Emily Eden

Mamma says she was then the prettiest, silliest, most affected husband-hunting butterfly she ever remembers ... and she has stiffened into the most perpendicular, precise, taciturn piece of "single blessedness" that ever existed, and that, till *Pride and Prejudice* showed what a precious gem was hidden in that unbending case, she was no more regarded in society than a poker or a fire-screen ... The case is very different now: she is still a poker — but a poker of whom everyone is afraid.

Mary Russell Mitford on Jane Austen

Beverley, the feeling went, had the outlook of a New Zealand sheep-farmer's wife — which was what she had been born to, after all — all practicalities and no panache.

Fay Weldon

Bimbos ...

A senescent bimbo with a lust for home furnishings.
Barbara Ehrenreich on Nancy Reagan

A face unclouded by thought.
Lillian Hellman on Norma Shearer

If people think I'm a dumb blonde because of the way I look, then they're dumber than they think I am.
Dolly Parton

HIMBOS

How often the Gods endow a man with a perfect profile and no brains to live up to it!
Katherine Mansfield

His shallowness was as sparkling as the surface of a rivulet.
Mary Braddon

Clifford is much improved in looks but in conversation he really is nothing and his constant little nervous laugh makes even his silence appear less negative than that of another person.
Lady Harriet Leveson Gower, describing Augustus Clifford Foster

Socrates must must been very tiresome when one thinks of it.
Ouida

A village explainer, excellent if you were a village, but if you were not, not.

Gertrude Stein on Ezra Pound

I discovered Rabelais, and thought him an obscure and limited bore. I'm quite certain that if I wanted to be indecent I could be more original than that.

Rachel Ferguson

[Walt] Whitman was like a prophet straying in a fog and shouting half-truths with a voice of great trumpets. He was seeking something, but he never knew quite what, and he never found it.

Amy Lowell

Mr Thayer's latest work is called, with that simplicity which is the gaudiest flower of pretentiousness, *An American Girl*.

Dorothy Parker

Mr Tellegen's English is of the fanciest persuasion; it even includes such refinements as the exquisite participle "gotten".

Dorothy Parker, reviewing Lou Tellegen's memoirs, Women Have Been Kind

Roland has the inner life of a tree, or possibly of a stump.

Margaret Atwood

And it is that word "hummy," my darling, that marks the first place in *The House at Pooh Corner*, at which Tonstant Weader Fwowed up.

> *Dorothy Parker, reviewing A.A. Milne's*
> The House at Pooh Corner

Bob is not of a suspicious nature, but he can add two and two together. He has been doing that little dreary sum all the last ten days, till his head aches.

> *Rhoda Broughton*

He was a man who liked to hear himself talk, and who could talk pretty well, in rather a superficial manner, about any thing and every thing. He had your true talker's instinctive faculty for discovering a good listener.

> *Mary Braddon*

He left a bad taste in my mind.

> *Geraldine Endsor Jewsbury*

Hugh never thought it necessary to lower his voice when he said anything tender. The expression "love whisper" never could be applied to his amatory commonplaces; love-shout or love-bellow would be more applicable.

> *Rhoda Broughton*

Brief Encounters

Brief Encounters

I have only been mildly bored.

> Gertrude Atherton to Ambrose Bierce,
> after an argument of fierce literary debate

"Well, Nell," said she, presenting her cool peach cheek to me, "how are you? Much the same as usual, I see — hair arranged with a pitchfork and dress with a view to ventilation."

> Rhoda Broughton

"You're quite tall," Mrs Stone said.
I didn't say anything. I didn't say, And you're quite old. Or,
Your teeth are quite yellow and your paintings are quite nuts.

> Amy Bloom

"Oh, has Whistler's mother gone?"

> Dorothy Parker on Tallulah Bankhead, after the latter had to
> leave a party where she had been, on her own admission
> "noisy, tight and obstreperous"

Perhaps the Majors and Blairs and all the power-dressers of Britain should take the advice of Wallis Simpson to the Queen Mother who, when asked how she could best promote British fashion abroad, replied crisply: "Stay at home."

> from The Wit and Wisdom of the Royal Family

[When the American actress Jean Harlow pronounced her name "Margott"]: "No, no, Jean. The 't' is silent as in Harlow."

> Margot Asquith

A checkroom girl took one look at all the diamonds I was wearing and exclaimed, "Goodness, what beautiful diamonds."
"Goodness had nothing to do with it, dearie," I replied.

Mae West

Oh dear me — it's too late to do anything but accept you and love you — but when you were quite a little boy somebody ought to have said "hush" just once!

Mrs Patrick Campbell to George Bernard Shaw

When Dorothy Parker met Clare Boothe Luce in a doorway, Booth Luce made way saying "Age before Beauty."
Parker swept ahead, saying "Pearls before Swine."

Ava Gardner once approached Bette Davis in a hotel in Madrid.
She told Davis: "I'm Ava Gardner and I'm a great fan of yours."
Davis replied: "Of course you are my dear, of course you are."

from Movie Talk

Critic: She has made a full confession of her past life to her new husband. What honesty! What courage!
Miss Barrymore: What a memory!

Exchange regarding an unnamed actress

I noticed but eight chairs in her dining room. I remarked about this to her, as it was then the custom to give large and formal dinners.

"Yes, Miss de Wolfe," she replied, "there are but eight people in the whole of New York whom I care to have dine with me."

Elsie de Wolfe on Edith Wharton

"Girls! Girls! Put some pep into your work. How would you act, for instance, if I told you that all of your salaries were to be raised?"

"I would drop dead."

Theatrical impresario De Wolfe Hopper's first encounter with Edna Wallace

Once, the prime minister Mrs Thatcher and the Queen found themselves wearing almost identical outfits. Mrs Thatcher afterwards sent a memo to the Palace, suggesting that it might be a good idea if she could be given advance warning of the Queen's outfits on occasions when they were to meet, to avoid future embarrassment. Relations between the two women were said to be cool. A memo was returned by Buckingham Palace: "The Queen does not notice what other people are wearing."

from The Wit and Wisdom of the Royal Family

A very pretty but silly and loquacious woman complained to Madame Marie de Sévigné that she was being tormented by her admirers who stared at her whenever she appeared. Madame de Sévigné replied: "Oh Madame, it would be so easy for you to get rid of them. You have only to speak."

Anne Mathews

When she was described as being kind to her inferiors:
"Wherever does she find them?"

Dorothy Parker on Clare Boothe Luce

"You have your points, Gertrude, and I can't help liking you,
but I am free to say that I was never so glad to see the last of
any one in my life. I think you are headed straight for the
devil, but I shall pray for you."

*Gertrude Atherton's Aunt Mary on bidding
her teenage charge farewell*

When Noël Coward wanted to leave a party unfashionably
early, he told his hostess, Tallulah Bankhead: "I must think of
my youth."
She replied: "Well, next time, bring him along!"

Bette Davis

Charles R. Thorne, New York actor, to Rose Eytinge, his
leading lady, who yawned at the climax of one of his
anecdotes: "For heaven's sake, Rose, don't swallow me!"
Her response: "You forget, Mr Thorne, that I am a Jewess."

Two rival opera-singers in San Francisco, Adelina Patti and
Etelka Gerster, each hated to hear the other praised. When
an admirer of Patti's commented on the singer's remarkable
ear, Gerster replied: "Yes, she has two remarkable ears; in fact,
it is only justice to call them wings."

The comedienne Della Fox was served a lobster without a claw at a Baltimore restaurant. When she complained, the waiter explained that the lobsters had been fighting in their basket before being served, and hers had lost its claw in the battle.

"Take this lobster out immediately," replied Miss Fox, "and bring me the winner!"

Mrs Greeley greeted Margaret Fuller's outstretched hand with horror. "Ugh! Skin of a beast!" she cried, recoiling from Fuller's kid gloves.

Fuller asked to see what kind of gloves Mrs Greeley herself saw fit to wear.

"Silk," said Mrs Greeley, with satisfaction.

Fuller replied: "Ugh! entrails of a worm! entrails of a worm!"

Beatrice Lillie, on meeting Hermione Gingold in Piccadilly: "What a divine hat! I love the white bird nesting on those red and blue flowers. Only you could get away with it — or could you?" The bird was in fact a racing pigeon which had landed on the actress's head.

Hollywood
& beyond

Hollywood

STAR TURNS

Hollywood is Hollywood. Vulgarity was invented for those people!

Marlene Dietrich

The only "ism" Hollywood believes in is plagiarism.

Dorothy Parker

People who make movies know less about love than people who pay good money to see them.

Carol Shields

The studios were giant factories turning out the same length of scented tripe, dressed up with the same rubber stamp features of large cow-like heads, mammary glands, and ten-foot-high close-ups of nostrils you could drive a Cadillac into.

Mae West

I used to wonder if there wasn't a sub-species of womankind that bred children for the sole purpose of dragging them to Hollywood.

Hedda Hopper

Actresses will happen in the best regulated families.

Ethel Watts Mumford

It was a dull week in Hollywood when my engagement wasn't announced to one man or another.

Tallulah Bankhead

Let any pretty girl announce a divorce in Hollywood and the wolves come running. Fresh meat for the beast, and they are always hungry.

Hedy Lamarr

Making pictures, for an actress, is like betting, for a gambler. Each time you make a picture you try to analyse why you won or lost.

Hedy Lamarr

What must one do to receive an Oscar? Play Biblical characters, priests, or victims of sad and tragic disabilities … The more tragic the disability, the greater the chance of grabbing an Oscar.

Marlene Dietrich

I've done everything in the theatre except marry the property man.

Fanny Brice

Katharine Hepburn ran the whole gamut of emotions from A to B.

Dorothy Parker

She sounds more and more like Donald Duck.

Bette Davis on Katharine Hepburn

Rock Hudson [is] the only man I know who can answer "yes" or "no" (and not a word more) to questions like "how many films have you made?"

Jean Rook

Hollywood

Interviewing Bette Davis ... is the nearest I've come to dying of fright.

Jean Rook

Zsa Zsa Gabor ... is thirty-eight for publication, fifty-five for real, fifty-seven to her enemies, and fifty-nine according to the US newspaper she's threatening to sue.

Jean Rook

My mother was the stage mother of all time. She really was a witch. If I had a stomach-ache and didn't want to go on, she'd say, "Get out on that stage or I'll wrap you around a bedpost."

Judy Garland

Their love scenes were like hot fat on an iron griddle.
Hedda Hopper on Clark Gable and Norma Shearer

Clark looked every inch the truck driver.
Hedda Hopper on Clark Gable

You've probably heard of Louella. The writer of a syndicated screen column of the Hearst newspapers, she terrorized most of Hollywood, was flatteringly called "The Gay Illiterate".
Tallulah Bankhead on Louella Parsons

If I'm not convinced that what I do is great entertainment, I would rather do nothing at all but sit at home and polish my diamonds.

Mae West

She drags feminism along casually in her slinking stride like a cave woman who has just killed her dinner ... And most importantly, she still looks like a whore and thinks like a pimp.

Julie Burchill on Madonna

If Madonna is the scourge of young womanhood, then young womanhood is sillier than I thought.

Anna Raeburn

I really wanted to be the new Shirley Temple.

Madonna

Miss Welch tottered by, clad in a brown jersey dress that appeared to be on the inside of her skin ...

Maureen Lipman on Raquel Welch

Many people found her a strange cold fish of a woman.

Lana Turner on Laraine Day

Mamie [Van Doren] often acted like Mr Ed the Talking Horse and some say she was the forerunner of the Farrah Fawcett school of acting.

Paula Yates

Trying for the mystery of glamour, Julie Andrews merely coarsens her shining nice-girl image, becoming a nasty Girl Guide.

Pauline Kael

Glamour is what Julie Andrews doesn't have. She does her duties efficiently but mechanically, like an airline stewardess.

Pauline Kael

He was an aloof, remote person, intent on being Cary Grant playing Cary Grant playing Cary Grant.

Frances Farmer

Ethel has no superior as a witherer.

Tallulah Bankhead on Ethel Barrymore

Claudette Colbert ... had some difficult angles to her face ... The right side of her face was called "the other side of the moon" because nobody ever saw it.

Mary Astor

The best time I ever had with Joan Crawford was when I pushed her down the stairs in *What Ever Happened to Baby Jane?*

Bette Davis

She's the most completely starlike star we have, working at it twenty-four hours a day.

Hedda Hopper on Joan Crawford

Hollywood's first case of syphilis! Now, you mustn't print that.

Bette Davis on Joan Crawford

Poor Joan. I wish I could have liked her more.
Bette Davis on Joan Crawford

She was good at what she did, at what she settled for.
Bette Davis on Joan Crawford

She built a career out of a set of mannerisms instead of real acting ability. Take away the pop-eyes, the cigarette and those funny clipped words and what have you got?
Joan Crawford on Bette Davis

Some of my best leading men have been horses and dogs.
Elizabeth Taylor

Dear Elizabeth Taylor, I owe a lot to you. Love, Joanie.
Joan Rivers, who made the actress the butt of her jokes for years

She was adorable! Such a shame she grew up. And out.
Bette Davis on Shirley Temple

Men don't really believe that women exist. Marilyn Monroe died of this.
Lucy Ellmann

Marilyn used to bicycle about the studio with a volume of Euclid under her arm, in a pathetic attempt to make Arthur Miller think she was studious.
Anita Loos on Marilyn Monroe

She was extremely adept at wiggling her ass and batting her eyelashes.

Zsa Zsa Gabor on Marilyn Monroe

No one could catch the elusive Greg Bautzer until Dana Wynter came along and married him. How she did it, none of us can figure out to this day. After all, he not only had the milk free, as the saying goes, but the cream and the cow as well.

Lana Turner

As for Howard Hughes, I found him likeable enough, but not especially stimulating. In our most personal conversations, he confessed his preference for oral sex. I wasn't interested, but that didn't seem to bother him.

Lana Turner

Mildred's beauty had the purity of an advertisement for bottled spring water, and she produced thoughts that were like bubbles.

Anita Loos on Mildred Harris, Charlie Chaplin's wife

But her favourite form of exercise was walking off a movie set, which she did with the insouciance of a little girl playing hopscotch.

Anita Loos on Louise Brooks

In spite of all this ballyhoo about Tallulah the Mysterious, Tallulah the Exotic, I'm just a good healthy girl with a husky voice and the strength of a horse.

Tallulah Bankhead

I'll submit to wheedling, but never to bulldozing. The man doesn't live who can bludgeon me into a contract …
Tallulah Bankhead

Smaller feet would look silly on a girl of her height.
Marie Dressler on Greta Garbo

Forget all the bilge about Garbo. She's excessively shy. When at ease with people who do not look upon her as something begat by the Sphinx and Frigga, Norse goddess of the sky, she can be as much fun as the next gal.
Tallulah Bankhead on Greta Garbo

Garbo will be forgotten in ten years.
Clare Boothe Luce in 1932

You sordid fool — get the tears!
Tallulah Bankhead, being photographed by a Life *reporter while in an emotional embrace with her friend, Hedda Hopper*

She was perfectly beautiful, and bound to succeed. She left no stone unturned, no lever unused.
Hedda Hopper on Tallulah Bankhead

Hate from Miss Bankhead is a small badge of honour, and praise undesirable. Miss Bankhead will never act in a play of mine again, only because I can stand only a certain amount of boredom.
Lillian Hellman, regarding Tallulah Bankhead's performance in The Little Foxes *in 1939*

I can outshout any producer in Hollywood.

Hedda Hopper

Inasmuch as I left home to escape the heritage of being a butcher's daughter, it seems ironical that I was to spend the rest of my life in dealing in ham.

Hedda Hopper

Poor thing, she was in everybody's movies. Never had one of her own.

Bette Davis on Hedda Hopper

Dramatic art in her opinion is knowing how to fill a sweater.

Bette Davis on Jayne Mansfield

You should cross yourself when you say his name.

Marlene Dietrich on Orson Welles

It's like meeting God without dying.

Dorothy Parker on Orson Welles

What kind of whore part do I play next?

Jean Harlow, to her agent, after the screening of Red Dust

Poor Rudy groped his way through many a love scene, I mean really groped.

The actress Nita Naldi, referring to the fact that both she and Rudolph Valentino were terribly short-sighted

[Montgomery Clift] is the only person I know who's in worse shape than I am.

Marilyn Monroe

[Laurence Olivier] gave me the dirtiest looks, even when he was smiling.

Marilyn Monroe

[Tony Curtis] only said that about "kissing Hitler" because I wore prettier dresses than he did.

Marilyn Monroe

Errol would have screwed anything that moved.

Bette Davis on Errol Flynn

I always knew Frank [Sinatra] would wind up in bed with a boy.

Ava Gardner, referring to Mia Farrow

I daresay when Swanson's eighty-five she'll be doing another come-back in a wheel chair. She has the will and the intestinal fortitude to push through all obstacles.

Hedda Hopper on Gloria Swanson

As I say, with this Dietrich, if you ever saw her in those pre-Sternberg films, she was just a galloping cow.

Louise Brooks

Hollywood

Mr Stewart Grainger appears as Paganini and pretends to play the violin. There is something agricultural about Mr Grainger's fiddling. He appears to be sawing wood with one hand and milking a cow with the other.

Elspeth Grand

It's a new low for actresses when you have to wonder what's between her ears instead of her legs.

Katharine Hepburn on Sharon Stone

The little Mexican Lupe had attracted favourable attention from Doug Fairbanks, who had put her in one of his pictures. On location one day a horse bit her. Lupe turned round and bit the horse. That was the kind of a girl she was.

Hedda Hopper on Lupe Velez

The trouble is, when he puts his arm around me I feel like a horse.

Clara Bow on Gary Cooper

Actors like him are good but on the whole I do not enjoy actors who seek to commune with their armpits, so to speak.

Greer Garson on Marlon Brando

Evelyn's idea of acting was to march into a scene, spread her legs and stand flat-footed and read her lines with masculine defiance.

Louise Brooks on Evelyn Brent

They should give Haber open-heart surgery — and go in
through the feet.

> *Julie Andrews on gossip columnist Joyce Haber*

Helen Dunbar was cast in the role of the dowager aunt.
Helen Dunbar. She had been there when the egg cracked
open and I emerged.

> *Gloria Swanson*

Lily wasn't exactly a beauty, though her eyes were; she just
happened to be born in a day when standards were far lower
and less exacting.

> *Rachel Ferguson on Lily Langtry*

She was her customary self, as amiable as an adder.

> *Helen Lawrenson on Ava Gardner*

She looked as though butter wouldn't melt in her mouth —
or anywhere else.

> *Elsa Lanchester on Maureen O'Hara*

Thelma Ritter — nobody played a better servant.

> *Bette Davis*

Clara Bow, for God's sake, she was a half-witted little girl, her
father was a busboy, her mother was in a nuthouse, and she
wasn't bright.

> *Louise Brooks*

She was the kind of girl you'd always known, only you'd never known she was that kind of girl.

Adela Rogers St John on Clara Bow

I think I shall risk the halibut. It can't be too awful, can it? After you've lived with Laurence Harvey, nothing in life is ever really too awful again.

Hermione Baddeley on Laurence Harvey

… a face that looks like it's been dipped in wax.

Bette Davis on Merle Oberon

She was there when they invented the original close-up!

Bette Davis on Mary Pickford

PRIMA DONNAS

It does no harm to the ego to be worshipped.

Mae West

To be a star is to own the world and all the people in it.

Hedy Lamarr

I won't be happy until I'm as famous as God.

Madonna

I knew I had always been too cute for my own good, too sexy, that I could always get what I wanted.

Margaret Trudeau

Hollywood

I think the measure of your success to a certain extent will be the amount of things written about you that aren't true.

Cybill Shepherd

I detest humanity. I'm allergic to it.

Brigitte Bardot

I'm so popular it's scary sometimes. I suppose I'm just everybody's type.

Catherine Deneuve

Actors cannot choose the manner in which they are born. Consequently, it is the one gesture in their lives completely devoid of self-consciousness.

Helen Hayes

The theatre is a gross art, built in sweeps and over-emphasis.

Enid Bagnold

I am Alicia Lamour, the recluse chanteuse.

Alice Kahn

If I'm such a legend, then why am I so lonely?

Judy Garland

I wish I could be a human being sometimes. I would avoid certain situations.

Maria Callas

The press doesn't believe you have any feelings. They sure don't believe in the Bible.

Hillary Rodham Clinton

I think people can tell that we're not up our own bottoms.
Spice Girl Mel Brown

Like most comediennes, I always yearned to writhe and weep my way across a stage.

Marie Dressler

God ... what is normal? Is it normal to work in McDonald's? Is it normal to be a star?

k. d. lang

I never felt like one of those movie queens they used to manufacture in Hollywood. I had sexy genes, I guess, and that helped.

Rita Hayworth

I watched the big women stars and enjoyed Sarah Bernhardt on a bill. She had a clause in her contract forbidding animal acts to play with her, but she permitted W. C. Fields.

Mae West

I'm glad you like my Catherine. I like her too. She ruled thirty million people and had three thousand lovers. I do the best I can in two hours.

Mae West, her speech from the stage following her performance in Catherine the Great

Miss Bara was Pestilence herself, her monumental
wickedness would not have been tolerated by Caligula in his
beatnik depths for one moment.
Bette Davis on Theda Bara

You have to admit that most women who have done something with their lives have been disliked by almost everyone.
Françoise Gilot

I knew I belonged to the public and to the world, not
because I was talented or even beautiful, but because I had
never belonged to anything or anyone else.
Marilyn Monroe

I'm always the heroine of whatever I think about.
Cher

I am not interested in money. I just want to be wonderful.
Marilyn Monroe

All I desire is Fame, and fame is nothing but a great noise.
Margaret Cavendish, Duchess of Newcastle

Admiration from unknown persons leaves me cold.
Marlene Dietrich

The marble — it is too shiny ...
*Greta Garbo, to Jack Gilbert, when he commissioned a $15,000
black marble bathroom to entice her to marry him. He had the
builders back to flute the marble with chisels*

Hisdemeanours
&
Missdemeanours

CASANOVAS

The only original thing about some men is original sin.
Helen Rowland

Anyone who believes that only time will tell has never been in a boy's locker room.
Joan Rivers

When men speak over-quick and over-fair, what is that but the toadstool that springs from their breath?
Ouida

To most men "repentance" is merely the interval between the headache and the next temptation.
Helen Rowland

Man's subconscious mind still feels that there is not the same dishonour in lying to a woman as in lying to a man.
Elinor Glyn

Familiarity breeds attempt.
Jane Ace

Behold, in matters of love, a woman is a specialist, but a man is a general practitioner.
Helen Rowland

Give a man a free hand and he'll run it all over you.
Mae West

Sidi's youthful appetite for life … has taken less than forty-eight hours to give him a farmer's tan, broiled cheeks and a vermilion nose. Last night he went all alone to the carnival, amused himself like a god, and came home at 5 a.m., ravished and satiated at having clasped so many anonymous behinds.

Colette on her second husband, Henry de Jouvenel

"Have a care, my dear!" said she, smiling, "it is sometimes dangerous to make requests to men, who are too desirous of receiving them."

Fanny Burney

He liked to out-Herod Herod, and his reputation for unscrupulous vice was as dear to him as though it had been the fame of the soldier or the statesman; he loved his mere approach to damn a woman's character …

Ouida

"Off! do not touch me!" cried Alma, fiercely, as his hand wandered towards the delicate form that he could crush in his grasp as a tiger's fangs a young gazelle. "Your words are shame, your love pollution, your presence hateful!"

Ouida

Nothing annoys a man as much as to hear a woman promising to love him "forever" when he merely wanted her to love him for a few weeks.

Helen Rowland

"What was he doing with your hand?" pursued my father, still more severely.
"I'm sure I don't know," stammered I.

Rhoda Broughton

Men are creatures with two legs and eight hands.

Jayne Mansfield

People have often said that we put Mama up on a pedestal, to which I always reply, "Shoot, that's the only way we could keep Daddy away from her!"

Dolly Parton

A man's heart is like a barber shop in which the cry is always, "NEXT!"

Helen Rowland

A fox is a wolf who sends flowers.

Ruth Weston

The trouble with Ian is that he gets off with women because he can't get on with them.

Rosamund Lehman on Ian Fleming

Don't accept rides from strange men, and remember that all men are strange as hell.

Robin Morgan

Now it so happened, that one of the inimitable Fitzroy's peculiarities was, that he could never be in love with the same woman for more than three months at a time.

The Hon. Mrs Norton

A Bachelor of Arts is one who makes love to a lot of women, and yet has the art to remain a bachelor.

Helen Rowland

Womanhood was a difficult thing to get a grip on in those hills, unless you were a man.

Dolly Parton on her rustic childhood

A man may be guilty of stealing a girl's heart, but he always feels hurt and indignant if she refuses to take it back again after he has finished with it.

Helen Rowland

MEN'S AFFAIRS

When will I understand that what's astonishing about the number of men who remain faithful is not that it's so small but that there are any of them at all?

Nora Ephron

Other Women have to listen to more maudlin and dishonest tales from husbands about their wives' shortcomings than they ever willingly elicit, and few gambits are more repulsive.

Germaine Greer

No doubt, even Solomon told each of his seven hundred wives that he had merely thought he loved the others, but that she was the only girl he "ever really cared for" in just that way.

Helen Rowland

If you're married for more than ten minutes, you're going to have to forgive somebody for something.

Hillary Rodham Clinton

The most common cause of impotence is marriage to other women. The penis knows its ten commandments, and this is its own, quirky way of slapping its owner's hand.

Cynthia Heimel

Let it first be established that more sagging husbands fancy unattached women than are fancied by them.

Germaine Greer

Married men inevitably say that their wives don't understand them, they haven't been sleeping together for ten years, they're not going to leave their wives until their children grow up and they've never felt this way about another woman. Women, who would otherwise laugh out loud at their friends were they to volunteer this same information, believe them.

Paula Yates

Whatever your age, a man can leave you for another woman or die (of the two, I think dying is preferable).

Helen Gurley Brown

A man can have a love affair that means no more to him than a good meal.

Barbara Cartland

Somehow, the moment a man has surrendered the key of his heart to a woman, he begins to think about changing the lock.

Helen Rowland

PERVERSION

That's definitely the trouble with upper-class Englishmen — they just can't drive past a perversion without pulling over.

Kathy Lette

Too many of these guys are working things out in the bedroom that still belong on the football field.

Laura Chester

All men worth having in bed are partly beasts.

Erica Jong

Men love any underwear that's easy to get off.

Jo Brand

Men who tell you they read the "Ann Summers" catalogue for the articles are lying.

Rita Rudner

"What Have You Got on Your Hip? You Don't Seem to
Bulge Where a Gentleman Ought To."

Irene Franklin — title of her banned song,
referring to man carrying a hip flask

Somehow, just at the psychological moment when a
bachelor fancies that he is going to die for love of a woman,
another woman always comes along and interrupts him.

Helen Rowland

MISSDEMEANOURS

I used to be Snow White … but I drifted.

Mae West

I moved to Los Angeles when I was twenty-one. I felt like a
kid in a candy shop. I'd be driving down the road and —
Mmmm! There was a guy and Mmmm! There was a guy!

Tori Amos

It was such a surprise that one could attract. It was like a
stream finding out that it could move a rock.

Enid Bagnold

No girl was ever led down the primrose path who hadn't
charted the road.

Doris Lilly

There are things I'm grateful I didn't do. Like sleep with two bisexual models at the same time! They were so gorgeous and I wanted to be the baloney in between the wholewheat bread.

Tori Amos

Dolly has a most reprehensible style of dancing ... Dolly is the sort of woman, upon whom Mr Algernon Swinburne would write pages of magnificent uncleanness.

Rhoda Broughton

God and I have a great relationship, but we both see other people.

Dolly Parton

My big fantasy is to seduce a priest.

Linda Ronstadt

As an actress I felt I had to know all about men, the wonderful monsters ... I took various boys around the house to show off our furniture. We had no etchings.

Mae West

NYMPHOS

In my heart of hearts, I always know that God comes first. But in my body of bodies, some urges can be absolutely irresistible.

Dolly Parton

"Put It On, Take It Off, Wrap It Up, Take It Home, Good Night, Call Again."

Belle Baker — song title

Never put off for tomorrow who you can put out for tonight.

Joan Rivers' fictional character, Heidi Abromowitz

It must have been great fun to make love to me. I was so pathetically easy.

Marie Dressler

She's had more hands up her dress than the Muppets.

Joan Rivers on her fictional character, Heidi Abromowitz

One has a kind of honey. But not for bees.

Enid Bagnold

As a baby, so family lore went, I only smiled when a male bent over my baby carriage.

Zsa Zsa Gabor

There is sex without love, and, no, hair doesn't grow out of your fingertips when it happens!

Helen Gurley Brown

If all those sweet young things were laid end to end, I wouldn't be at all surprised.

Dorothy Parker on the girls at the Yale Prom

Sometimes it seems to me I've known so many men that the FBI ought to come to me first to compare fingerprints.

Mae West

Life is too short to waste on the admiration of one man.

Rose Scott

[Mlle de Beaumenard, who had many lovers and married relatively late] — very like a weathercock, and did not become fixed till she was rusty.

Sophie Arnould

I feel like a million tonight, but one at a time.

Mae West

The devil and I certainly had one thing in common: we were both horny.

Dolly Parton

My friends all seem incapable of keeping their hands on their ha'pennies for longer than three hours and their idea of being aloof is making him wait till after the pudding.

Paula Yates

I'll flirt with anybody, from the garbage man to grandmothers.

Madonna

They used to say that I was a slut, a pig, an easy lay, a sex
bomb, Minnie Mouse or even Marlene Dietrich's daughter,
but I'd rather say that I'm just a hyperactive adult.

Madonna

She's the original good time that was had by all.
Bette Davis on an unnamed starlet

A great actress from the waist down.
Dame Margaret Kendal on Sarah Bernhardt

You know, she speaks eighteen languages, but she can't say
"No" in any of them.
Dorothy Parker speaking of an acquaintance

"I Want to Do All Day, What I Do All Night."
song title as quoted by Mae West

On being told that ten men were waiting to meet her at her
home: "I'm tired, send one of them home."
Mae West

Her legs were apart so often they were pen pals.
Joan Rivers on her fictional character, Heidi Abromowitz

Women feel licensed to behave with the sexual opportunism
that was once considered the particular characteristic of
men. The family gamekeeper has turned poacher.
Melanie Phillips

I hate to tell you how old I am, but I reached the age of consent 75,000 consents ago.

Shelley Winters

Men aren't attracted to me by my mind. They're attracted by what I don't mind.

Gypsy Rose Lee

The resistance of a woman is not always a proof of her virtue, but more frequently of her experience.

Ninon de Lenclos

Boys, to put you at your ease, let me just say that at our all-girl gatherings, we don't just talk about length … we also talk about width.

Kathy Lette

My mind's so broad, a double decker bus could make a U-turn in it.

Jean Rook

PAST IT

Getting down to your last man must be as bad as getting down to your last dollar.

Mae West

Women give themselves to God when the devil wants nothing more to do with them.

Sophie Arnould

"I May Be Getting Older Every Day (But Getting Younger Every Night)."

Sophie Tucker — song title

There is actually no age limit to being a slag, it just gets sadder as you get older.

Jenny Eclair

The pure-bred siren is as extinct these days as the great white auk.

Anita Loos

FOR MONEY

You gotta get up early in the morning to catch a fox and stay up late at night to get a mink.

Mae West

Lunch at the Ritz is always a decisive moment. At this time of the day, women are ready to make concessions and to think over their plans.

Marlene Dietrich

A poor woman should never be so improvident as to give away what she could sell.

Germaine Greer

When the chips are down, every woman must realize she is sitting on her fortune.

Germaine Greer

If a man sends me flowers, I always look to see if a diamond bracelet is hidden among the blossoms. If there isn't one, I don't see the point of the flowers.

Hedy Lamarr

Money can't buy love, but it can definitely rent by the hour.

Kathy Lette

Losing my virginity? I thought of it as a career move.

Madonna

Jackie Onassis was one smart woman, believe me. She knew. God gave women sex so we can shop the next day.

Joan Rivers

Honey, if you are going to fuck for a dime, you can't complain because somebody else is getting a fur coat.

Florynce R. Kennedy

Virtue has its own reward and no sale at the box office.

Mae West

She's not a hooker, she's more of a cab-fare girl. "I'll get home, fine, just give me a hundred dollars."

Rona Jaffe on her fictional character, Melba Toast

"Who Paid the Rent for Mrs Rip Van Winkle While Rip Van Winkle Was Away?"

Sophie Tucker — song title

"There's Company in the Parlour, Girls, Come on Down."
Sophie Tucker — song title

People knew a man by the company he kept, but they generally knew a woman by the man who kept her.
Lisa Alther

WOMEN'S AFFAIRS

I could be such a wonderful wife to another wife's husband.
Judith Viorst

Mrs West was with her, who is a great prude, having but two lovers at a time; I think those are Lord Haddington and Mr Lindsay, the one for use, the one for show.
Lady Mary Wortley Montagu

Now and then your Other Woman does fancy somebody's husband, but she usually cares only to borrow him for a night or two.
Germaine Greer

The real issue may be that monogamy is not terribly realistic.
Rita Mae Brown

The Frenchwoman prides herself on being thought unfaithful to her husband; the Englishwoman on being thought faithful to him; but though their theories are different, their practice comes to much the same thing.
Ouida

Missdemeanours

Dear Princess Bibesco
I am afraid you must stop writing these little love letters to
my husband while he and I live together. It is one of the
things which is not done in our world ... Please do not
make me have to write to you again. I do not like scolding
people and I simply hate having to teach them manners.

Katherine Mansfield

When feeling cheap and nasty, remind yourself that without
infidelity, literature and opera would be up shit creek.

Kathy Lette

I say I don't sleep with married men, but what I mean is that
I don't sleep with happily married men.

Britt Ekland

Bad Behaviour

Bad Behaviour

Sometimes you have to be a bitch to get things done.

Madonna

Life's a bitch and then they call you one.

Mary Frances Connelly

Women are labelled as bitches if we're in any way assertive
and so we go around pretending we're these vapid creatures
who don't have a dark side. Every single month I'm a total
bitch for at least a week of it.

Siobhan Fahey

I found my inner-bitch and ran with her.

Courtney Love

A bitch loves being born. It's her first experience of making
another woman scream and cry.

Pamela Stephenson

A bitch is more memorable than a sweet housewife.

Bette Davis

"It Takes A Good Girl To Be Bad."

Sophie Tucker, song title

It is possible, after all, to be too good.

Ruth W. Grant

Bad Behaviour

If I'd observed all the rules, I'd never have got anywhere.
Marilyn Monroe

If I were well behaved, I'd die of boredom.
Tallulah Bankhead

The trouble with trouble is it starts out as fun.
Naomi Judd

I delight in sinning and have to compose a mask.
Sulpicia

Really, there is very little temptation to be moral in this world.
Geraldine Endsor Jewsbury

What do you mean by my "irrational and inarticulate passions"? All my passions are perfectly reasonable and only inarticulate when they are thought unreasonable.
Vanessa Bell

She's the kind of girl who climbed the ladder of success, wrong by wrong.
Mae West

Forget the psychiatry. Bottling It Up Is Best. Every time. So you die a little younger, what the hell? At least you get a bigger crowd at your funeral.
Maureen Lipman

Bad Behaviour

I do not want reverence; it goes to passion's funeral. And I do not want to be good either, for that means a person knowing all her own possibilities and limits.

Mrs W. K. Clifford

Between two evils, I always pick the one I never tried before.

Mae West

Now that women have been more or less freed by the three C's — cars, can-openers, and contraceptives — it seems too bad that the fourth one, Conscience, so often has to butt in.

Peg Bracken

I've seen things, and that's almost the same as doing them.

Loretta Lynn

There's nothing more dangerous than someone who thinks of himself as a victim. Victims feel it's within their rights to fuck over everyone.

Cynthia Heimel

Good manners are good morals in detail.

Anne Mathews

I hardly know any annoyance so deeply repugnant to English feelings, as the incessant, remorseless spitting of Americans.

Frances Trollope

Ultimately, the lower middle classes are the most deviant.
That's why they have net curtains; they have things to hide,
the weirdos.

Jenny Eclair

It is a superficial world one lives in, and superficial
understandings suit it best, so *vive la bagatelle.*

Elizabeth Carter

"Well if I'm dysfunctional, who dysfuncted me?"

Kathy Lette

You live but once, you might as well be amusing.

Coco Chanel

I'm no angel but I'm no Bo-Peep either.

Princess Margaret

To vice, innocence must always seem only a superior kind of
chicanery.

Ouida

Instant gratification takes too long.

Carrie Fisher

Have you ever heard a man or woman say, "I was wrong"?
Hardly.

Rita Mae Brown

Bad Behaviour

There is very little pure blue blood left in this country, as most of it is tainted with cocaine.

Jenny Eclair

FAME

What a pity people will not fulfil their destiny, and stay in their own proper niche in this world's gallery!

Fanny Fern

Keep a diary and someday it'll keep you.

Mae West

Pop music is just hard work, long hours and a lot of drugs.

Mama Cass Elliot

What I got kicked out of school for, it's the same thing I see myself doing on stage now.

Rickie Lee Jones

To be on the cover of a magazine these days, you have to have been through drug rehab three times. What message is this giving young people?

Mary Lou Retton

Fame is so desirable that ordinary individuals will often submit to any humiliation in order to achieve it.

Celia Brayfield

Most people are such Egotists that they are incased in their own selves, as if they were in Gelatin Overalls.
Lady Ottoline Morrell

RUDENESS

Her servants walk a perpetual plank.
Hedda Hopper on Joan Crawford

He couldn't see a belt without hitting below it.
Margot Asquith on David Lloyd George

Like everyone else these days I'm haircuttist, jacketist, small dickist when judging male drivers.
Isla Dewar

Any woman who can't say a four-letter word sometimes is deceitful.
Fanny Brice

Of all the Royals, Anne is the rudest. If anyone crosses her, she lays back her ears, bares her teeth, and kicks them to splinters.
Jean Rook

I despise the pleasure of pleasing people whom I despise.
Lady Mary Wortley Montagu

Bad Behaviour

Next time you encounter a nasty salesperson, be Katharine Hepburn.

Elizabeth Hilts

Rudeness is annoying, but offended flouncing is worse, being so dreadfully conceited.

Alice Thomas Ellis

Do I worry about my image as the sharpest-toothed, longest-tongued and clawed, most relentlessly snappish bitch in British journalism? No.

Jean Rook

A little humour leavens the lump.

Dorothy Parker

That institution, the morning paper propped up against the coffee-pot, may be all very well for the reader, but it hardly adds to the comfort of those who have to eat their bacon in its shadow.

Diana Woods

Fashions in sin change.

Lillian Hellman

The older one grows the more one likes indecency.

Virginia Woolf

My virtue's still far too small, I don't trot it out and about yet.

Colette

When women go wrong, men go right after them.

Mae West

If ... you can't be a good example, then you'll just have to be a horrible warning.

Catherine Aird

Men bestow compliments only on women who deserve none.

Madame Bachi

LYING

Women and children cry out of spite.

Lady Caroline Lamb

Actions lie louder than words.

Carolyn Wells

GOSSIP

People got snoopy so I told them lies to hear their tongues wag. The women are all snakes and none of them I can call friends.

Calamity Jane

Gossip is the opiate of the oppressed.

Erica Jong

It is said that nothing gives a brighter glow to the complexion, or makes the eyes of a beautiful woman sparkle so intensely, as triumph over another.

Lady Caroline Lamb

She dealt her pretty words like blades,
As glittering they shone,
And every one unbared a nerve
Or wantoned with a bone.

Emily Dickinson

I hate to spread rumours — but what else can one do with them?

Amanda Lear

Do send me some gossip. It would be like water to a fish.

Virginia Woolf

SPECIFIC

I don't care if people say I'm a bitch or I'm obnoxious, 'cos I am.

Courtney Love

In your dangerous path of life you have almost unavoidably amassed a great deal of useless trash — gathered weeds instead of flowers.

Lady Georgiana Spencer

Bad Behaviour

My mind was early opened to Lady Elizabeth's character, unparalleled I do believe for want of principle and delicacy, and more perverted than deceitful, for I really believe she hardly herself knows the difference between right and wrong now.

Lady Harriet Leveson Gower

I really look upon her in every light as the most dangerous devil.

Lady Lavinia Spencer on Lady Elizabeth Foster

If I weren't Jean Rook, I'd be nervous of Jean Rook.

Jean Rook

She is toujours Lady Spencer, Vanity and bragging will not leave her, she lugg'd in by the head and shoulders that she had been at Windsor.

Lady Mary Coke on Lady Georgiana Spencer

I must go and see what that poor gaping imbecile my charwoman is doing about dinner.

Virginia Woolf

Henry VIII, or King Syphilis Gut Bucket Wife Murderer VIII as I prefer to call him, was born in 1491.

Jo Brand

I'm just a little Jewish girl trying to be cute.

Dorothy Parker

Bad Behaviour

When someone walks down the aisle and says to you, "Is someone sitting there?" just say, "No one — except the Lord."

Carol Leifer

My Lady Stafford and myself waited for you three hours. Three hours of expectation is no small trial of patience, and I believe some of your martyrs have been canonized for suffering less.

Lady Mary Wortley Montagu

I give you my brow which you brutalized in such a cowardly way. Perhaps your kisses will revive my love. I doubt it.

Sarah Bernhardt

I am invariably late for appointments — sometimes as much as two hours. I've tried to change my ways but the things that make me late are too strong and too pleasing.

Marilyn Monroe

"Take Lady Calantha then," exclaimed Lady Margaret, with assumed calmness, while every furious passion shook her frame; "and may she prove a serpent to your bosom, and blast the peace of your whole family." "She is an angel!" exclaimed the Admiral, "and she will be our pride, and our comfort." "She is a woman," returned Lady Margaret, with a malicious sneer; "and, by one means or other, she will work her calling."

Lady Caroline Lamb

His character seems to me a parallel with that of Caligula;
and had he had the same power, would have made the same
use of it.

Lady Mary Wortley Montagu on Dean Swift

How Mlle. Pinard screamed when she found her powder-
puff full of wood lice! — it served her right for her
Frenchified ways, Humpo said, with that subtle satiric wit
that distinguished him even at that age.

Mary Dunn

His general preaching against money was meant to induce
people to throw it away, that he might pick it up.

Lady Mary Wortley Montagu on Alexander Pope

SWEET REVENGE

One must be a woman to know how to revenge.

Madame de Rieux

My whole career has been an act of revenge.

Ruby Wax

Enemies to me are the sauce piquant to my dish of life.

Elsa Maxwell

The feminine faculty of anticipating or inventing what can
and will happen is acute, and almost unknown to men. A
woman knows all about a crime she may possibly commit.

Colette

Revenge is sweet. Sweeter than tiramisu.

Kathy Lette

My fame has enabled me to torture more formidable men.

Sharon Stone

I am brought to bed of a son, who shall suck hatred to you with his milk, and that I intend to have a great many more, for the sole purpose of raising you up enemies.

Marie de Sévigné

If life is not always poetical, it is at least metrical.

Alice Meynell

When this judge let a rapist go because the woman had been wearing a miniskirt and so was "asking for it" I thought, ladies, what we all should do is this: next time we see an ugly guy on the street, shoot him. After all, he knew he was ugly when he left the house. He was asking for it.

Ellen Cleghorn

The harder they hit, the more encouraged I get.

Hillary Rodham Clinton

Milk is the stuff of vengeance and full fat ripens best — especially when it is tipped on to a carpet or, better still, the floor of the car.

Belinda Hadden and Amanda Christie

Remember, if you write anything nasty about me, I'll come round and blow up your toilet.

Courtney Love

If you want to get revenge on a man, marry him!

Belinda Hadden and Amanda Christie

God will protect us. But to make sure, carry a heavy club.

Gypsy Rose Lee's mother's advice to her children

Post something appropriate to your adversary. We know of one woman who posted her erstwhile lover an anchovy.

Belinda Hadden and Amanda Christie

Her silences are organic bickerings.

Djuna Barnes on Mary "Mother" Jones

I like your Plan immensely of Extirpating that vile race of beings call'd man but I (who you know am clever (VERREE) clever) have thought of an improvement in the sistim suppose we were to Cut of [sic] their prominent members and by that means render them Harmless innofencive Little Creatures; We might have such charming vocal Music Every house might be Qualified to get up an opera and Piccinis Music would be still more in vogue than it is & we might make such usefull Animals of them in other Respects Consider Well this scheme.

Maria Allen

It is normal to want to ram his car if he and his new girlfriend have been spotted in it.

Helen Lederer

Don't waste time trying to break a man's heart; be satisfied if you can just manage to chip it in a brand new place.

Helen Rowland

When I think that you are being untrue to me with women, I have murder in my heart.

Aline Bernstein

VICTIMS

Round her dear little white throat hung a gold locket, in which lurked the photograph of the latest victim.

Rhoda Broughton

When he is late for dinner and I know he must be either having an affair or lying dead on the street, I always hope he's dead.

Judith Viorst

Once, when I noted that "the Queen needs her straggly eyebrows trimming" (she still does), readers wrote back suggesting that mine should be trimmed with an axe.

Jean Rook

Yet this heroine of a humble, every-day tragedy contrived to look cheerful. The world — the sniffing, feminine world, particularly — must not rejoice in her downfall.

Ella Hepworth Dixon

HYPOCRISY

Only my dogs will not betray me.

Maria Callas

If we are fed on innocuous platitudes we cannot develop either mentally or morally.

Katharine Hepburn

As to telling the truth, every one would be so disillusioned and my life would seem so banal, that I prefer to cling to my legends.

Gabrielle Chanel

Charity is the sterilized milk of human kindness.

Ethel Watts Mumford

What has always puzzled me is why the English, who are so profoundly honest, write the best novels about thieves, crooks, and lurid murderers.

Elsa Schiaparelli

It is extremely tacky for a friend to mention a friend's weight to her face. Behind her back is a different thing altogether.

Cynthia Heimel

Gratitude is such an unpleasant quality, you know; there is always a grudge behind it.

Ouida

You can tell the person who lives for others by the haunted look on the faces of the others.

Katharine Whitehorn

A bad woman always has something she regards as a curse — a real bit of goodness hidden away somewhere.

Lady Troubridge

Women who are content with light and easily broken ties do not act as I have done. They obtain what they desire and are still invited to dinner.

George Eliot, referring to her life with George Lewes

The rising executives who accustom themselves to *haute cuisine* at the firm's expense have wives at home feasting uncomplainingly on baked beans on toast.

Germaine Greer

Sara could commit adultery at one end and weep for her sins at the other, and enjoy both operations at once.

Joyce Cary

A tangled fishnet of contradictions: she liked the rich because she liked the way they looked, their clothes, the things in their houses, and she disliked them with an open and baiting contempt; she believed in socialism but seldom, except in the sticky sentimental minutes, could stand the sight of a working radical.

Lillian Hellman on Dorothy Parker

He liked women to pray. Religion had gone with his other ideals, but it was a beautiful thing in a woman.

Gertrude Atherton

Every word she writes is a lie, including "and" and "the".

Mary McCarthy on Lillian Hellman

Say anything you like, but don't say I love to work. That sounds like Mary Pickford, that prissy bitch!

Mabel Normand

Lady Elizabeth Foster is here all in a tender wee waw high ho! sort of mood with coquettish weeds and *demi caractère* grief, agreeable and pleasant enough I think when she forgets to Devonsherise her mouth.

Lady Crewe commenting on Lady Foster's feigned grief after the death of her estranged husband.

239, 273, 279, 290
Schillinger, Liesl 230
Schlafly, Phyllis 35
Schreiner, Olive 68
Schulder, Diane B. 36
Scott, Rose 161
Scudéry, Madeleine de 88
Segal, Naomi 8, 21, 35, 74
Sévigné, Charles de 25
Sévigné, Marie de 12, 68, 108, 130, 182, 220, 223, 272, 294, 298, 302
Shakespeare, William 257
Shaw, George Bernard 129
Shaywitz, Sally E. 2
Shearer, Norma 124, 136
Shelley, Mary 110, 112, 121, 122, 285
Shepherd, Cybill 147
Shields, Carol 8, 134
Siddons, Sarah 230
Simpson, Wallis 128
Sinatra, Frnak 143
Sitwell, Edith 121, 122, 230, 256
Skinner, Cornelia Otis 121, 293
Slick, Grace 194
Smith, Bessie 7, 56
Smith, Dodie 110
Smith, Stevie 81
Solanas, Valerie 24, 37
Spark, Muriel 58
Spencer, Lady Georgiana 179, 180
Spencer, Lady Lavinia 179
Staël, Germaine de 56, 287
Stanford, Sally 52
Stark, Freya 117
Stasi, Linda 199
Stead, Christina 279
Stein, Gertrude 120, 125

Steinem, Gloria 34, 100, 115, 213, 241, 293
Stephenson, Pamela 96, 107, 170
Stepney, Jack 205
Stevenson, Helen 56, 59, 62, 211, 212, 234, 247
Stone, Sharon 144, 182
Sullivan, Sheila 44
Sulpicia 171
Swanson, Gloria 143, 145, 301
Swift, Dean 24, 181
Sybil, Orfea 56

T-shirt slogan 48
Taylor, Elizabeth 139
Tellegen, Lou 125
Temple, Shirley 139
Tenuta, Judy 48
Thatcher, Margaret 130, 246, 247, 248
Thomas, Irene 84
Thorne, Charles R. 131
Thrale, Hester 94, 109, 230
Todd, Dorothy 214
Tolstoy, Sophie 84
Tomlin, Lily 42, 290, 291
Townsend, Sue 78, 192, 201, 258
Trapido, Barbara 278
Tremain, Rose 257
Tristan, Flora 277
Trollope, Frances 173, 273, 274, 282, 283
Troubridge, Lady 186
Trudeau, Margaret 146
Truss, Lynne 47, 59, 240
Truth, Sojourner 34, 35, 249
Tucker, Sophie 4, 53, 164, 165, 166, 171, 277
Turnbull, Margaret 95
Turner, Lana 137, 140, 290
Tweedie, Jill 38, 49, 244

Ulrich, Mabel 242
Unknown author 102

Vail, Amanda 6
Valentino, Rudolph 142
Valois, Marguerite de 115
Van Demen, Bella 71
Van Doren, Mamie 78, 137, 302
Velez, Lupe 144
Vestris, Madame 192
Vigée-Le Brun, Elizabeth Louise 208
Viorst, Judith 54, 95, 166, 185, 204, 220, 243, 249
Vokes, May 117
Vreeland, Diana 192, 213, 215, 223, 224, 249, 292

Walker, Mrs 266
Wallace, Edna 130
Wasteneys, Lady 119
Wax, Ruby 182, 280
Webb, Mary 24, 254
Welch, Raquel 137, 244
Weldon, Fay 84, 95, 123
Welles, Orson 142
Wells, Carolyn 89, 178, 276
West, Mae 3, 6, 8, 33, 39, 48, 53, 81, 87, 109, 129, 134, 136, 146, 148, 152, 158, 159, 161, 162, 163, 164, 165, 172, 174, 177, 190, 191, 195, 228, 248, 285
West, Rebecca 246
Westheimer, Dr Ruth 59, 64
Westley, Helen 252
Weston, Ruth 154
Wharton, Edith 14, 75, 108, 130, 190, 205, 222, 266
Whitcher, Frances Miriam 294

Index

Whitehorn, Katharine
25, 36, 60, 77, 106, 186,
192, 223, 225, 239, 243
Whitman, Walt 125
Whitton, Charlotte 3, 31
Williams, Zoe 119
Winfrey, Oprah 28, 54,
56, 73, 191
Winters, Shelley 163
The Wit and Wisdom of
the Royal Family 128,
130, 202
Wolff, Isabel 118, 191,
255, 257
Wollstonecraft, Mary 68,
82
Wolstenholme, Suzanne
14
Women's liberation
slogan 34
Wood, Victoria 194, 222,
224, 275, 276
Woods, Diana 30, 101,
177, 258, 269
Woods, Vicki 85
Woolf, Virginia 3, 18,
108, 109, 118, 177, 179,
180, 207, 214, 219, 230,
256, 277, 303
Woolley, Hannah 4, 30
Wynter, Dana 140

Yates, Paula 12, 61, 77,
116, 137, 156, 161, 217
Yonge, Charlotte 228

Work, Power &
Money

Life is a do-it-yourself kit, so do it yourself. Work. Practice.

Phyllis Diller

Too many people seem to think life is a spectator sport.

Katharine Hepburn

No great talker ever did any great thing yet, in this world.

Ouida

There's no sauce for play like work.

Edna Ferber

Let others name the limits of your capabilities. For your own part, refuse to consider limits.

Marie Dressler

But there, that's life; one day you're drinking the wine and the next day you're peeling the grapes and someone's calling you "Beulah".

Julie Burchill

Life should consist in at least fifty per cent pure waste of time, and the rest in doing what you please.

Isabel Paterson

It is not true that life is one damn thing after another — it's one damn thing over and over.

Edna St Vincent Millay

This is the day of instant genius. Everybody starts at the top, and then has the problem of staying there.

Helen Hayes

I yield to no one in my admiration for the office as a social centre, but it's no place actually to get any work done.

Katharine Whitehorn

Routine and details have always avoided me.

Elsa Schiaparelli

I work in chaos. My desk, as I survey it from my vantage point, looks like a still life from Hieronymus Bosch.

Maureen Lipman

There is a time for work. And a time for love. That leaves no other time.

Coco Chanel

You have to be patient. I'm not.

Madonna

Divorcing a career is not unlike divorcing a husband; you have to find another meal ticket.

Barbara Howars

I prepare myself for rehearsals like I would for marriage.

Maria Callas

Work, Power & Money

Power is sweet, and when you are a little clerk you love its sweetness quite as much as if you were an emperor, and maybe you love it a good deal more.

Ouida

There are people who will tell you that no girl possessing a grain of common sense and a little nerve need go hungry, no matter how great the city. Don't you believe them.

Edna Ferber

My ideal existence is summed up by the following: a lovely padded rut with a salary at one end and a pension at the other.

Joyce Grenfell

I am ambitious. But if I weren't as talented as I am ambitious I would be a gross monstrosity. I am not surprised by my success because it feels natural.

Madonna

The main advantage of working at home is that you get to find out what cats really do all day.

Lynne Truss

It's sexy to be competent.

Letty Cottin Pogrebin

Most men have learned to enjoy loving a doer rather than a dodo.

Helen Gurley Brown

Woman's place is in the home, and that's where she should go just as soon as she gets done at the office.

Anonymous

How to distinguish between a rut and a groove and an intelligent pattern?

Peg Bracken

Ambition is a far surer guarantee of female chastity than virtue ever was.

Julie Burchill

As for not sleeping with the boss, why discriminate against him?

Helen Gurley Brown

There are very few jobs that actually require a penis or a vagina. All other jobs should be open to everybody.

Florynce R. Kennedy

I have yet to hear a man ask for advice on how to combine marriage and a career.

Gloria Steinem

The only jobs for which no man is qualified are human incubators and wet nurse. Likewise, the only job for which no woman is or can be qualified is sperm donor.

Wilma Scott Heide

But oh, what a woman I should be if an able young man would consecrate his life to me as secretaries and technicians do to their men employers.

Mabel Ulrich

Powerful men often succeed through the help of their wives. Powerful women only succeed in spite of their husbands.

Linda Lee-Potter

To a woman, just the satisfaction of knowing that she is self-supporting turns her crust into angel's food.

Dorothy Dix

People often say, "My but the little vixen has a lot of energy", mostly because I never shut up.

Bette Midler

Tough On Black Asses
  Jackie "Moms" Mabley's explanation of the real meaning of the initials TOBA (Theatre Owners' Booking Association)

I've never worked so hard in my life … I'm glad I took care of myself as a little girl.
  American comedienne Joan Davis, speaking about the long hours she worked on her TV series I Married Joan

Chanel was a workaholic. She must have had a lot to forget.

Marlene Dietrich

The idle never stick to their arrangements.

Julia Darling

I mean what's so fulfilling about fulfilment anyway?

Maureen Lipman

Nothing that is worthwhile is ever easy.

Indira Gandhi

The beaten track does not lead to new pastures.

Indira Gandhi

I believe if I were locked in a windowless room with a deadline I would spend the time trying to tunnel out rather than get on with it.

Alice Thomas Ellis

Late birds get worms while early birds get tired.

Judith Viorst

The more a thing is filed away, the more totally useless it is. A sweet disorder in the desk at least ensures that the whole thing is ploughed through often enough for useful things to come to the surface.

Katharine Whitehorn

My life is not up for criticism, just my work.

Cher

If I ever get to heaven, I'll be stuck making manna in the Holy Kitchens and putti-sitting fat feathered babies quicker than I can say Saint Peter.
Jill Tweedie's fictional character, Martha the Fainthearted Feminist

I always heard that genius is something that they beat to death first with sticks and stones, and set up on a great rock to worship afterwards.

Ouida

Behind every successful man is a woman with a brush and shovel cleaning up the shit he's too full of himself to notice.
Isla Dewar

A career is erotically sexual, it's my real passion. A career is like always having a mistress on the side.

Raquel Welch

I was never impressed by my work.

Marlene Dietrich

If I love my profession, it is perhaps because it takes the place of all the talents I lack.

Gabrielle Chanel

The progressive disqualification of women for exciting and responsible positions in industry or the professions begins as soon as they are born.

Germaine Greer

It is only very recently that women have succeeded in entering those professions which, as Muses, they typified for the Greeks.

Miriam Beard

Who knows what women's intelligence will contribute when it can be nourished without denying love?

Betty Friedan

Men don't really like women and that is really why they don't employ them. Women don't really like women either, and they too can usually be relied on to employ men in preference to women.

Germaine Greer

A career is wonderful, but you can't curl up with a career on a cold night.

Marilyn Monroe

POLITICS AND POWER

His delivery at the dispatch-box has all the bite of a rubber duck.

Marcia Falkender on John Moore

Running for office is the least aerobic of the socially interactive sports.

Carrie Fisher

I amuses me to know that I am emotionally ready to handle power and I no longer want it.

Barbara Howars

I still think [Margaret Thatcher] should be strung up by the bollocks.

Jo Brand

The reason there are so few female politicians is that it is too much trouble to put make-up on two faces.

Maureen Murphy

Sport has been called the last bastion of male domination. Unfortunately, there are others — Congress, for instance.

Mariah Burton Nelson

Group conformity scares the pants off me because it's so often a prelude to cruelty towards anyone who doesn't want to — or can't — join the Big Parade.

Bette Midler

People call me a feminist whenever I express sentiments that differentiate me from a doormat or a prostitute.

Rebecca West

In politics, if you want anything said, ask a man; if you want anything done, ask a woman.

Margaret Thatcher

Politics are usually the executive expression of human immaturity.

Vera Brittain

In politics women ... type the letters, lick the stamps, distribute the pamphlets and get out the vote. Men get elected.

Clare Boothe Luce

I don't mind how much my ministers talk — as long as they do what I say.

Margaret Thatcher

[Margaret Thatcher] surprised everyone by buying a house in Dulwich instead of moving to Bolivia with the rest of the Nazis.

Jo Brand

Mrs Clinton's shown the way to power is paved with matrimony.

Helen Stevenson

I'm way too honest to go into politics.

Cher

Say what you like about Genghis Kahn but, when he was around, old ladies could walk the streets of Mongolia at night.

Jo Brand

Adolf Hitler was stamping his feet and chewing rugs (so they said) in the German chancellery in Berlin. To show-people he was a ham actor and a talented local murderer.

Mae West

I never talk politics, not only from hating them but from every person one speaks to having seven different opinions.

Lady Georgiana Spencer

Mr Winston Churchill ... a notorious weathercock in his utterances on votes for women (and much else!).

Sylvia Pankhurst

Voting for [Margaret Thatcher] was like buying a Vera Lynn LP, getting it home and finding "Never Mind the Bollocks" inside the red, white and blue sleeve.

Julie Burchill

Either liberty is a false ideal and men should stop dying for it, or the men who are against it in peacetimes should be assassinated before they may build up ripened wars.

Genêt

Knowledge is power — if you know it about the right person.

Ethel Watts Mumford

Powerful women are either sexually voracious rulers, like Catherine the Great or Elizabeth I, or treacherous bitches like Cleopatra or Helen of Troy.

Celia Brayfield

I don't read such small stuff as letters, I read men and nations. I can see through a millstone, though I can't see through a spelling-book.

Sojourner Truth

MONEY

Laughter is the pauper's money.

Djuna Barnes

We begin life with loss. We are cast from the womb without an apartment, a charge plate, a job or a car.

Judith Viorst

Things were simpler all round then ... taxes were something only dogs had to pay.

Hedda Hopper

Manners maketh man, but they don't seem to make money, and the saying that politeness always pays is one of the fifty-odd biggest lies I know.

Rachel Ferguson

When they want to overpay you, there's usually a reason.

Diana Vreeland

It's amazing how healing money can be.

Dolly Parton

The most popular labour-saving device is still money.

Phyllis George

The Arts

THE ARTS

If you have a burning, restless urge to write or paint, simply eat something sweet and the feeling will pass.

Fran Lebowitz

I understood that the muse was not an angel. She was a tease.

Alice Kahn

I have the conviction that excessive literary production is a social offence.

George Eliot

Publishing is a marketplace, not a meritocracy.

Alice Kahn

New books are like young girls — fit for nothing.

Helen Westley

How I loathe the kind of novel which is about a lot of sisters.

Rachel Ferguson

More unwholesome, wet blanket, lachrymose, diluted, Rosa-Matilda sort of products than these modern insipidities, in three volumes, cannot exist.

Augusta Johnstone on novels

Editors are supersmart, the only people smart enough to understand how stupid and shallow the readers are.

Alice Kahn

I've been sick of writing, and everything connected with literature or improvement of the mind; to say nothing of deep hatred of my species about whom I was obliged to write as if I loved 'em.

Mrs Gaskell

The worst thing that can happen to a writer is to become a Writer.

Mary McCarthy

I'm making more money vertically than I used to make horizontally.

Xaviera Hollander, referring to her novel The Happy Hooker

The fact is, writing can be done only during the time when one ought to be doing something else.

Isabel Paterson

I have yet to meet a writer who wouldn't rather peel a banana than apply himself to the pen.

Alice Thomas Ellis

Writers are selfish people, with a love of their own company so passionate that it seems entirely likely that one day one of us just might get ourselves pregnant.

Julie Burchill

People who push their poems into their autobiographies are perhaps doubtful whether they can publish them any other way.

Enid Bagnold

CRITICS

I saw editors as the people who cut all the good stuff out of my stories.

Alice Kahn

Everything considered, *Joceleyn* is, in my opinion, a bad production. Commonplace thoughts, false sentimentality, loose style, obsolete and diffuse verse, subject flat, personages dragging on everywhere, affectation united to negligence ... To sum up, it is a pity that Lamartine wrote *Joceleyn*, but it's lucky for the publisher that *Joceleyn* was written by Lamartine.

George Sand

Humour is snooted upon, in a dignified manner, by the lofty-minded.

Dorothy Parker

The book was one of those affected by Mrs Marston and her kind. It had no relation whatever to life. Its ideals, characters, ethics and crises made up an unearthly whole, which, being entirely useless as a tonic or as a balm, was so much poison.

Mary Webb

Most editors love spunk — especially in a woman. What they don't like is a woman with balls.

Alice Kahn

The prose is not so much deathless, as lifeless, the characters
so flat they might have been cut from the back of a
cornflakes box.

Isabel Wolff

When Women write, the Criticks, now-a-days,
Are ready, e'er they see, to damn their Plays,
Wit, as the Men's Prerogative, they claim,
And with one Voice, the bold Invader blame.

Mary Davys

My literary reputation — or rather the lack of it — is the
work of male reviewers who fear female sexuality and don't
like successful women.

Erica Jong

In nineteen-twentieths of the book I think we may delight
and rejoice; and I heartily wish you joy of it.

Harriet Martineau

I've always thought that "proof" copies of books were so
called because here at last is the proof you've always wanted
that X can't write for shit.

Julie Burchill

I am obnoxious to each carping tongue
Who says my hand a needle better fits,
A Poet's pen all scorn I should thus wrong,
For such despite they cast on Female wits:
If what I do prove well, it won't advance,
They'll say it's stolen, or else it was by chance.

Anne Bradstreet

SPECIFIC WRITERS

Justly famed for her critiques, her poisonous impeachments
of her sex, Dotty Parker is the mistress of the verbal grenade.

Tallulah Bankhead

I enjoyed talking to her, but thought nothing of her writing.
I considered her "a beautiful little knitter".

Edith Sitwell on Virginia Woolf

Fate has not been kind to Mrs Browning. Nobody reads her,
nobody discusses her, nobody troubles to put her in her
place.

Virginia Woolf on Elizabeth Barrett Browning

Oh! Mr Thackeray! I ought to have known from experience,
that beauty and brains never travel in company — but I was
disenchanted when I first saw your nose.

Fanny Fern

I have just read D. H. Lawrence's "Kangaroo". How I hated
it! ... full of Spite, bitterness, & nasty "cur" like snarley
feeling.

Lady Ottoline Morrell

It goes on for nearly three hundred pages, with both of them
vibrating away like steam launches.

Dorothy Parker on Ada Cleveland and
John Gaunt, the characters in Elinor Glyn's It

Anita Loos wrote in the vernacular of easy money.

Elizabeth Hawes

Oh God. I can't bear Sebastian Faulks. It's just Mills and Boon with guns!

Isabel Wolff

It is not long since the grave closed over George Eliot, or more properly speaking, Mary Ann Evans, and yet it has already been faintly whispered by some, and loudly asserted by others, that she has been greatly overrated.

Julia Clara Byrne

And as for Moore's *Principia Ethica* … It was drawing-room philosophy and no more use to anyone that those pairs of mantelpiece dogs with dead-looking eyes.

Rose Tremain

My relationship with William Shakespeare is best described as non-meaningful. By that, I mean he doesn't bother me and I don't bother him.

Maureen Lipman

Jane Austen's novels, which strangely retain their hold on the public taste, are tedious to those who dare to think for themselves.

Kate Sanborn

The Arts

READING

If there was graffiti in a lavatory cubicle I had to read every word, and sometimes even corrected the spelling and punctuation.

Sue Townsend

To save my mother from the electric chair, I couldn't read three pages of it.

Dorothy Parker on James Branch Cavell's The Silver Stallion

I always read the last page of a book first so that if I die before I finish I'll know how it turned out.

Nora Ephron

I was a print slut. I would read anything, anytime, anywhere: the *Beano*, the *Spectator* and the Kellogg's cereal packet.

Sue Townsend

Women read far more novels than men do. Also novels are growing more and more salacious. Can one fact be the result of the other?

Diana Woods

PAINTING

Remember I'm an artist. And you know what that means in a court of law. Next worst to an actress.

Joyce Cary

You got paid ten dollars an hour [for posing nude]. It was a dollar fifty at Burger King. I kept saying, "It's for Art."

Madonna

I felt encouraged by the advice of Winston Churchill, who used to say, "Don't be afraid of the canvas." I have now reached the point where the canvas is afraid of me.

Beatrice Lillie

I absolutely agree with you, too, about Manet and Renoir. Renoir — at the last — bores me. His feeling for flesh is a kind of super butcher's feeling about a lovely little cut of lamb.

Katherine Mansfield

DANCING

But modern dances look to me like a middle-aged workman trudging home after a night shift.

Rachel Ferguson

It puts me in mind of two dogs fighting for a bone.
Sophie Arnould on Mlle Guimard, a tall, thin dancer, performing the pas de trois with two male dancers

Sport

Men who have a thirty-six-televised-football-games-a-week-habit should be declared legally dead and their estates probated.

Erma Bombeck

Men hate to lose. I once beat my husband at tennis. I asked him, "Are we going to have sex again?" He said "Yes, but not with each other."

Rita Rudner

The woman sits, getting colder and colder, on a seat getting harder and harder, watching oafs getting muddier and muddier.

Virginia Graham

Weight-lifting apparatus is a curious phenomenon – machines invented to replicate the back-breaking manual labour the industrial revolution relieved us of.

Sue Grafton

Give a man a fish and he eats for the day. Teach him how to fish and you get rid of him all weekend.

Zenna Schaffer

Tennis stars are so highly strung they could play the ball off their nerves.

Jean Rook

The Stronger Women Get, The More Men Love Football.
Mariah Burton Nelson – book title

Golf is not a sport. Golf is men in ugly pants, walking.

Rosie O'Donnell

Footballers are miry gladiators whose sole purpose in life is to position a surrogate human head between two poles.

Elizabeth Hogg

About rodeo? See, the bull is not supposed to be your role model …

Annie Proulx

You know, I always thought we should organize a sexual Olympics. A gold medal for best all-round love-making, best rear entry, best blow job, longest distance for ejaculation … What's the discus compared to that?

Rita Mae Brown

When male golfers wiggle their feet to get their stance right they look exactly like cats preparing to pee.

Jilly Cooper

The first time I see a jogger smiling, I'll consider it.

Joan Rivers

Animals

Animals

Every year, back Spring comes, with the nasty little birds yapping their fool heads off, and the ground all mucked up with arbutus. Year after year.

Dorothy Parker

I'm the only woman in the world who can kick a giraffe in the face.

Tall comedienne Charlotte Greenwood

The only point in going to the zoo is to watch animals shag. Me, I'd boot out the giant pandas unless they started giving us our money's worth.

Jenny Eclair

We don't want beetroot-conditioner, we want peroxide and preferably peroxide that has been tested on small furry animals. If it doesn't blind rabbits then it's not strong enough.

Jenny Eclair

I believe in the total depravity of inanimate things.

Mrs Walker

If ants are such busy workers, how come they find time to go to all the picnics?

Marie Dressler

Mrs Peniston thought the country lonely and trees damp, and cherished a vague fear of meeting a bull.

Edith Wharton

Animals

Did you ever look through a microscope at a drop of pond water? You see plenty of love there. All the amoebae getting married.

Rose Macaulay

Any animal that walks and shits at the same time has got to be stupid.

Maria Callas on horses

If cats had slime or scales instead of fur there would be no gainsaying their utter nastiness.

Germaine Greer

The cat gives the world nothing and receives from it everything.

Georgina Stickland Gates

There is nothing sadder than hearing someone talking to their cat as if it were a real human being with a brain and a Marks and Spencer's charge card.

Jenny Eclair

My cat does not talk as respectfully to me as I do to her.

Colette

Cats only play the fool at certain times and I do not know the rules they play by.

Alice Thomas Ellis

Animals

Listen, cats ladder your tights and so they must die.

Jenny Eclair

If I were to make a cat book it would show the horribleness
of cats, their cruelty, their jealousy, their territoriality, their
utter lack of fine feeling, their abominable sex life.

Germaine Greer

Cats are too superior but at least their poo is small and neat;
dogs, on the other hand, do those massive meringue turds
bigger than your head.

Jenny Eclair

I can't understand why people throw sticks to dogs. Dogs
aren't particularly interested in sticks, what they are
interested in is crotches.

Jenny Eclair

Emotions are quite as detrimental to a dog's tail as they are to
a lady's complexion.

Ouida

I sometimes feel like shooting the Queen's corgis.

Princess Michael of Kent

Animals are my Best Friends. I adore dogs because they
accept me for myself. And, best of all, they do not read
newspapers.

Zola Budd

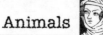

Dogs make shift with anything for love.

Enid Bagnold

Don't marry a man who has no time for dogs. Ten to one
such a man will only have time for himself.

Diana Woods

For sheer, unadulterated amusement, I recommend chicken
raising. As a means of increasing one's income, it is a doubtful
pastime, but for fun it can't be beat.

Marie Dressler

I think poultry have more humanity in them than any other
race, footed or feathered; and cocks certainly must have been
the first creatures that ever hit on the great art of advertising.

Ouida

Goldfish always die. To save time and effort, don't even
bother to decant them from the plastic bag.

Jenny Eclair

People & Places

TRAVEL

Travel, they say, broadens the mind but in my experience it is the other end of the anatomy that feels the effect.

Beatrice Lillie

Heaven permits the forgetfulness that the world may be peopled, and that folks may take journeys to Provence.

Marie de Sévigné

I couldn't bear the time on Board Ship — Wind Wind, & Stamping young women & badly made men, marching round & round the Decks, or lying with a silly novel or a 1930 Vol. of Punch — Asleep, Mouths open & large abdomens. I discovered that I had a terrible fountain of dislike in myself, which welled up & sprayed my fellow Passengers.

Lady Ottoline Morrell

What a pity when Christopher Columbus discovered America that he ever mentioned it.

Margot Asquith

New York … that unnatural city where everyone is an exile, none more so than the American.

Charlotte Perkins Gilman

August in New York is a month of such total, perfect vileness that most New Yorkers pretend it doesn't exist.

Rona Jaffe

The "simple" manner of living in Western America was more distasteful to me from its levelling effects on the manners of the people, than from the personal privations that it rendered necessary.

Frances Trollope

The social system of Mr Jefferson, if carried into effect, would make of mankind an unamalgamated mass of grating atoms, where the darling "I'm as good as you", would soon take the place of the law and the Gospel.

Frances Trollope

America, the magic dream of the world, holds out expectations beyond what can humanly be fulfilled.

Elsa Schiaparelli

In America, that polish which removes the coarser and rougher parts of our nature, is unknown and undreamed of.

Frances Trollope

Animal life is so infinitely abundant, and in forms so various, and so novel to European eyes, that it is absolutely necessary to divest oneself of all the petty terrors which the crawling, creeping, hopping, and buzzing tribes can inspire, before taking an American summer ramble.

Frances Trollope

All the freedom enjoyed in America, beyond what is enjoyed in England, is enjoyed solely by the disorderly at the expense of the orderly.

Frances Trollope

People & Places

It was no breach of decorum to speak of fleas in California, or even to scratch.

Gertrude Atherton

Notwithstanding all this, the country is a very fine country, well worth visiting for a thousand reasons; nine hundred and ninety-nine of these are reasons founded on admiration and respect; the thousandth is, that we shall feel the more contented with our own.

Frances Trollope

We lived on terms of primaeval intimacy with our cow.

Frances Trollope on life in America

I looked forward to arriving in Australia more than I had ever looked forward to anything — if you don't count getting my ears pierced.

Bette Midler

Melbourne is the kind of town that really makes you consider the question "Is there life before death?"

Bette Midler

I came to believe, in fact, that it is a crime to think in Australia.

Bette Midler

There is not food in Australia. Not as we know it. The natives do, of course, on occasion put matter to mouth, but one cannot possibly call what they ingest food.

Bette Midler

274

Canada is useful only to provide me with furs.

Madame de Pompadour

The longer I lived in Europe the firmer was my conclusion that the better class of Americans were the only people who had really fine table manners.

Gertrude Atherton

And what has China ever given the world? Can you really respect a nation that's never taken to cutlery?

Victoria Wood

In France ... there is always decadence, it is the great national genius and source of life. The French have, indeed, a natural aptitude for decadence; it is in them a sign of health.

Laura Riding

Pest was the most bustling city I had seen on the Continent, and reminded me of Chicago. It was also very advanced; a divorce could be procured in twenty-four hours.

Gertrude Atherton

In Iceland you're either normal, and you do a normal job and you do everything in a normal way, or you're a weirdo, the town freak.

Björk Gudmundsdottir

Are we going to the Lebanon? I've never been there. I've been to Debenhams lots of times, though.

Spice Girl Mel C

Paseo de la Reforma, the main street, is thirty-six miles long and every malodorous yard of it is traffic chaos.

Germaine Greer on Mexico City

Rome is a very loony city in every respect. One needs but spend an hour or two there to realize that Fellini makes documentaries.

Fran Lebowitz

Chernobyl looked nice in the brochure.

Victoria Wood

There is something in the handsome inexpressiveness of Swedish architecture and Swedish towns which suggests a very good-looking face without any eyebrows.

Margaret Halsey

England used to be such a lovely country.

Cynthia Heimel

In London I was shocked to learn the pubs close at eleven.

Tallulah Bankhead

[The British Museum] is as cold and forbidding as one of the Elgin Marbles, and it takes longer to get the book you ask for than to write one.

Carolyn Wells

Everything smacked of the ancient days, plumbing of 1492 vintage.

Sophie Tucker on London

In no country ... are the marriage laws so iniquitous as in England, and the conjugal relation, in consequence, so impaired.

Harriet Martineau

England is the seat of the most abominable despotism, where laws and prejudices submit women to the most revolting inequality!

Flora Tristan

Beauty in London is so cheap, and consequently so common to the men of fashion ... that they absolutely begin to fall in love with the ugly women, by way of change.

Elizabeth Inchbald

In this country there are only two seasons: winter and winter.

Shelagh Delaney, referring to England

Those comfortably padded lunatic asylums which are known, euphemistically, as the stately homes of England ...

Virginia Woolf

You can't get a bookcase in this country for love or money. They've filled them all with their hideous knick-knacks and they're NOT LETTING GO.

Lucy Ellmann on England

NATIONAL TYPES

Alas, poor foreigners. What do they know about tea?

Barbara Trapido

English

I never was intended for a miner, and you have to go into an Englishman's brain with a pick and shovel.

Gertrude Atherton

The English manners of real life are so negative and still as to present no visible or audible drama.

Alice Meynell

You can be broke with more dignity in London than any of the world's large cities. The British, with their beautiful manners, never ask a stranger embarrassing questions.

Elsa Maxwell

Englishmen seem to remain boys a long time and then to grow old all at once.

Gertrude Atherton

The University youth of Great Britain must take priggish-
ness in the regular course of measles, mumps, whooping-
cough, Public School wickedness, the overwhelming
discovery of his own importance as an atom of the British
Empire, and cynicism.

Gertrude Atherton

You ask me whether English husbands are, in general, *bons et
aimables? Pas du tout, ma chère; tout au contraire.* They are, as far
as I can judge from the specimens I have seen, the most
selfish beings imaginable.

Marguerite Blessington

"Pity them, the English are so poor now, the most
unfortunate people on earth," my papa says, "and yet they
cannot lose their pride, their tradition, their history."

Christina Stead

But to return to Lord Granby. He carried his length of limb
rather lankily, but he had a beautiful Christ-like face that
seemed curiously out of place in the British aristocracy.

Gertrude Atherton

I am just crazy about royalty, especially queens. Your Queen,
for example, Elizabeth the Second … My dears, she is the
whitest woman of them all. She makes us all feel like the
Third World.

Bette Midler

I dearly love them because they are mad, mad, mad.

Elsa Schiaparelli

... these English ... you make one perfectly normal request at a normal volume and they pucker their rectums.

Dawn French, Jennifer Saunders and Ruby Wax

But what makes a visiting American feel most helpless and lonely in England is ... the relative scarcity of laughter. You can get a kind of whinnying sound out of the well-bred English merely by saying that it is raining.

Margaret Halsey

The other English vice is building-on ... Few Englishmen can resist the temptation to fling out a wing here, throw up a turret there.

Alice Thomas Ellis

To say truth, there is no part of the world where our sex is treated with so much contempt as in England ... I think it the highest injustice our knowledge must rest concealed, and be as useless to the world as gold in the mine.

Mary Wortley Montagu

English women are elegant until they are ten years old.

Nancy Mitford

In Britain, an attractive woman is somehow suspect. If there is a talent as well it is overshadowed. Beauty and brains just can't be entertained; someone has been too extravagant.

Vivien Leigh

You cannot know an Englishwoman intimately — nor casually, for that matter — without being staggered occasionally.

Gertrude Atherton

The Lady Dorothy is the last earthly representative of certain crude but effective persons who raised England from a pup.

Margaret Halsey

Englishwomen, she had been told, were very much of a pattern — the result of centuries of breeding in uninterrupted conditions.

Gertrude Atherton

Whatever the rest of the world thinks of the English gentleman, the English lady regards him apprehensively as something between God and a goat, and equally formidable on both scores.

Margaret Halsey

Englishwomen's shoes look as if they had been made by someone who had often heard shoes described, but had never seen any.

Margaret Halsey

The Briton is so apt to think that "Familiarity Breeds Contempt" — it probably does in England, but in Paris one can chat with one's inferiors about all sorts of extraneous subjects.

Maude Annesley

Americans

No people appear more anxious to excite admiration and receive applause than the Americans, yet none take so little trouble, or make so few sacrifices to obtain it. This may answer among themselves, but it will not with the rest of the world.

Frances Trollope

And the most disagreeable part of the manners of the Americans is that you are called upon to admire and be surprised to such a degree that … I was perfectly worn out.

Margaret Hall

I certainly believe the women of America to be the handsomest in the world, but as surely do I believe that they are the least attractive.

Frances Trollope

I have seen many beautiful American women who had no beauty at all.

Gertrude Atherton

The women do not bear the test of evening dress.

Margaret Hall

I never saw an American man walk or stand well; notwithstanding their frequent militia drillings, they are nearly all hollow-chested and round-shouldered.

Frances Trollope

I very seldom, during my whole stay in the country, heard a sentence elegantly turned, and correctly pronounced from the lips of an American. There is always something either in the expression or the accent that jars the feelings and shocks the taste.

Frances Trollope

She is as prim as a bolster, as stiff as a ram-rod, as frigid as an icicle, and not even matrimony with a New Yorker could thaw her.

Fanny Fern on Boston women

[An Englishman] never overheard Americans conversing without the word DOLLAR being pronounced between them.

Frances Trollope

How DOES America live with itself? Just by FORGETTING itself? Like an incontinent old man: stinks but ain't sure WHY.

Lucy Ellmann

The Americans are remarkable organizers. And that's just their problem, they organize everything. Everything is planned, even orgasms!

Marlene Dietrich

Americans have two brains, one in the usual place, and the other where the heart should be.

Marlene Dietrich

I never saw an American gentleman in my life. They are a second-hand, pawnbrokers'-shop kind of nation — a nation without literature, without art, and totally unconscious of the beautiful nature by which they are surrounded.

Mary Russell Mitford

Englishmen are not so easy to manage as American men, but I believe that as soon as I understand Arthur I shall be able to manage him quite easily.

Gertrude Atherton

American men, as a group, seem to be interested in only two things, money and breasts.

Hedy Lamarr

An interviewer asked me what book I thought best represented the modern American woman. All I could think of to answer was: *Madame Bovary*.

Mary McCarthy

No one from Europe ever loves an American long.

Genêt

French

French people eat the most intricate entrails of everything from the horse to the snail.

M. E. K. Fisher

I've heard of old Frenchwomen doing odd things in that line; and the *goûter*! They generally begin such affairs with eating and drinking, I believe.

Charlotte Brontë

The French got a reputation for bedroom habits little better than a mink's.

Mae West

Their hair, too, dragged to the top of the head & then lifted to its height appeared as if each female wished to be a tower of Babel in herself ...

Mary Shelley on Parisian women

It's true that the French have a certain obsession with sex ... France is the thriftiest of all nations; to a Frenchman sex provides the most economical way to have fun.

Anita Loos

Apropos of countenances, I must tell you something of the French ladies. I have seen all the beauties, and such (I can't help making use of the coarse word) nauseous —, so fantastically absurd in their dress! so monstrously unnatural in their paint! their hair cut short and curled round their faces, loaded with powder that makes it look like white wool, and on their cheeks to their chins, unmercifully laid on, a shining red japan that glistens in a most flaming manner, that they seem to have no resemblance to human faces, and I am apt to believe took the first hint of their dress from a fair sheep newly raddled.

Lady Mary Wortley Montagu

... insidiously seductive, I think, is the glory of France, perhaps because it has always struck me as being perfectly humourless.

Jan Morris

Cubans

The Cubans have accepted that adultery is their national sport.

Germaine Greer

Their clothes, including their brassières, were all two or three sizes too small and flesh bulged everywhere.

Germaine Greer on Cuban women

Italians

My God, Italian men are handsome! They are the latin Masai. Perfect teeth, all of them.

Doris Lilly

And no matter how he tries, an Italian can't keep his hands off his tie or shirt cuffs which he constantly tugs to make just a little longer. Freudian movements, every one.

Doris Lilly

Where would a southern woman's happiness be if she married for love?

Norma Lorimer

Italian men dance with you as if they want to make love to
you and drive you as if they want to kill you.

Doris Lilly

It is not true that no Italian ever tells the truth ... but it is
sadly true that when one does he suffers for it.

Ouida

As a rule, the Sicilians love having their children
photographed by any passing stranger, and will often offer to
dress them up in their ugly bests for you to take a snap at.

Norma Lorimer

Germans

With the Germans — well, who ever guessed the age of a
German woman correctly? From the moment she screws up
her hair at the most unbecoming angle on her unbecoming
head, she might be any age that did not matter.

Norma Lorimer

There is nothing in the world that's heavier or more
stupefying in the moral and physical sense than the average
German.

Germaine de Staël

Belgians

In general the Continental, or at least the Belgian, old women permit themselves a license of manners, speech, and aspect such as our venerable grand-dames would recoil from as absolutely disreputable, and Madame Reuter's jolly face bore evidence that she was no exception to the rule of her country.

Charlotte Brontë

Not having seen any appearance of sensitiveness in any human face since my arrival in Belgium, I had begun to regard it almost as a fabulous quality.

Charlotte Brontë

Norwegians

Norwegian food is, I think, noticeably inferior to Swedish, though after we left Oslo it stopped tasting as if it had been made with the milk from porcupines.

Margaret Halsey

Irish

The Irish are impatient for eternity.

Djuna Barnes

Having the Vapours

After all, in private we're all misfits.

Lily Tomlin

The thing about happiness is that it doesn't help you to grow; only unhappiness does that.

Lana Turner

Perfect contentment can rarely be recognized. Maybe in Tibet. Maybe in toddlers.

Carrie Fisher

Psychoanalysis was intended to take the place of the confessional, and we call it science. Both methods have dangers … Psychoanalysis, on the other hand, is a peril, because it is openly exploited for money.

Elsa Schiaparelli

The truth is, everyone should clean up someone else's detritus, because he isn't emotionally attached to it.

Peg Bracken

I must be the last psycho-virgin in California. I've never been ested, encountered or even rolfed. Call me hardcore unevolved.

Alice Kahn

I think unconditional love is what a mother feels for her baby, and not what you should feel for yourself.

Helen Gurley Brown

Laughing at myself is what I do best. Lord knows I have had practice.

Barbara Howars

Laugh and the world laughs with you. Cry and you cry with your girlfriends.

Laurie Kuslansky

Your handkerchief is to wave, not to cry into.

The Queen, when still Princess Elizabeth, cautioning her sister Margaret when they said farewell to their parents who were to tour Canada

I believe that, as a rule, only women should cry. God knows we've got enough reasons to!

Julie Burchill

I've had heartaches, headaches, toothaches, earaches, and I've had a few pains in the ass; but I've survived to tell about it.

Dolly Parton

Things are going to get a lot worse before they get worse.

Lily Tomlin

Time doesn't heal all wounds … Over the years, the scars hurt as much as the wounds.

Marlene Dietrich

God is a consolation! Valium before Valium was invented.

Marlene Dietrich

You know it's a bad day when you wake up and the birds are singing Leonard Cohen numbers.

Jenny Eclair

Who can begin conventional amiability the first thing in the morning? It is the hour of savage instincts and natural tendencies.

Elizabeth von Arnim

At present my idea of a good work-out is a two-hour worry about the bags under my eyes.

Maureen Lipman

The biggest problem people have is leisure. Anybody can handle a jam-packed day.

Peg Bracken

Sometimes I think I'll give up trying, and just go completely Russian and sit on a stove and moan all day.

Dorothy Parker

What sells is hope.

Diana Vreeland

Having been unpopular in high school is not just cause for book publication.

Fran Lebowitz

Having the Vapours

Nothing is dearer to a woman than a nice long obstetrical chat.

Cornelia Otis Skinner

Every week, it seems, I hear a new gynaecological atrocity tale.

Nora Ephron

When I got married, I said to my therapist, "I want to do something creative." He said, "Why don't you have a baby?" I hope he's dead now.

Joy Behar

Cynicism is a good thing to have on the outside, but it's a terrible thing to have on the inside.

Courtney Love

There's nothing like a good heartbreak to get a good song.

k. d. lang

If it ain't broke, break it would seem to be my design for living.

Julie Burchill

Self-esteem isn't everything; it's just that there's nothing without it.

Gloria Steinem

Having the Vapours

Lady Colin was a great sufferer from rheumatism; when I met her she had just returned from being boiled out at Salsamaggiore.

Gertrude Atherton

No one knows less of the interior decorations of the human body than I.

Gertrude Atherton

People that do not read or work for a livelihood have many hours they know not how to employ, especially women, who commonly fall into vapours or something worse.

Lady Mary Wortley Montagu

Madame de Brissac was indisposed today; she lay in bed, looked very handsome, and was dressed in a manner fit to make conquests. Oh, how I wish you had but seen how prettily she managed her pains, her eyes, her arms, and her cries.

Marie de Sévigné

He was a wonderful hand to moralize, husband was, specially after he began to enjoy poor health.

Frances Miriam Whitcher

Jane Greely is sick with the quinzy — quite sick. Jane Gridley's husband is sick. "Mrs Skeeter" is very feeble, "can't bear Allopathic treatment, cant have Homeopathic" — don't want Hydropathic — Oh what a pickle she is in — shouldn't think she would deign to live — it is so decidedly vulgar!

Emily Dickinson

Having the Vapours

I don't think women outlive men, Doctor. It only seems longer.

Erma Bombeck

Elizabeth and I have been fully occupied. She has cried a great deal, fainted a good deal, and played the harp most of all.

Margaret Fuller

Learning how to knit was a snap. It was learning how to stop that nearly destroyed me.

Erma Bombeck

My Cousin Eliza is a young lady intended by nature to be a bouncing good-looking girl. Art has trained her to be a languishing affected piece of goods.

Charlotte Brontë

Solange is amusing with her pain in her heart or stomach. I fancy that the latter organ is the one that plays the most important part in her life.

George Sand, referring to her daughter

And how is Roger? Has he started any new disease?

Vanessa Bell, referring to her discarded lover, Roger Fry

Having the Vapours

Lady Honiton was about the most odious hypochondriac going, in a perpetual state of unremitting battle with the whole outer world in general, and allapathists, homeopathists, and hydropathists, in especial.

Ouida

The extreme delicacy of Miss Weston makes it prodigiously fatiguing to converse with her, as it is no little difficulty to keep pace with her refinement, in order to avoid shocking her by too obvious an inferiority in daintihood and ton.

Fanny Burney

Mrs Ford kept a convenient little fund of misery on hand, which she could draw upon at the shortest notice ... she was a woman full of anxieties who liked to have one within reach.

Margaret Oliphant

Mrs Tarlton was an invalid, and although patient, she met her acuter sufferings unresistingly.

Gertrude Atherton

Young ladies are delicate plants. They should take care of their health and their complexion. My dear, did you change your stockings?

Jane Austen

RIP

RIP

If I had any decency, I'd be dead. Most of my friends are.
Dorothy Parker

Life is too short. Death seizes us while we are still full of our miseries and our good intentions.
Marie de Sévigné

Only the young die good.
Ethel Watts Mumford

The good die young — but not always. The wicked prevail — but not consistently.
Helen Hayes

It takes eighty-two years to produce activity of the head with the inactivity of the hips. Upon thinkers, death steals from the feet up; upon laymen, from the head down.
Djuna Barnes

Growing old is just a matter of throwing life away back; so you finally forgive even those that you have not begun to forget.
Djuna Barnes

Death is not ours to deal.
Ouida

Death is just so out there right now. It's Linda. It's Gianni and Diana.
Sue Margolis

Life is painful, nasty and short … in my case it has only been painful and nasty.

Djuna Barnes

They say you shouldn't say nothing about the dead unless it's good. He's dead. Good.

Jackie "Moms" Mabley

Many suicides have greatly surprised me; I find life so very interesting.

George Eliot

The only way you can become a legend is in your coffin.

Bette Davis

I detest posterity.

Ouida

Dying's not so bad. At least I won't have to answer the telephone.

Rita Mae Brown

Death is so unnatural.

Enid Bagnold

Hospitals generally prefer people not to die in them. It disturbs the other patients and depresses the nurses.

Germaine Greer

Cremation … seemed more civilized and sanitary. Who
wants to be a worm's hamburger?

Rita Mae Brown

And when you die, have everything buried with you. If the
next wife wants it, make her dig. I'm going to have a
mausoleum. More closet space.

Joan Rivers

People like their blues singers dead.

Janis Joplin

Oblivion is the flower that grows best on graves.

George Sand

Sleep is death without the responsibility.

Fran Lebowitz

When I'm dead, they'll all have known me, you'll see!
They'll all have slept with me!

Marlene Dietrich

We are but skin about a wind, with muscles clenched against
mortality.

Djuna Barnes

In our family we don't divorce men — we bury them.

Ruth Gordon

The widow who considers with seriousness whether she will best express her sense of loss by a Marie Stuart cap or an Alsatian bow of tarlatan, is already half consoled.

Mrs Fanny Douglas

The young widow ... should, of course, never remain in mourning for her first husband after she has decided to be consoled by a second.

Emily Post

No sooner do I die, than all the flowers I have ever longed for in life pour in. Everyone says all of the nice things that I would so have loved to have repeated to me; my enemies and even my friends forgive me, charitable memories collect everything that is charming and overlook everything that is not — and why? Simply because I am no longer there to be made happy.

Elizabeth Bibesco

Excuse my dust.

Dorothy Parker

Life, the permission to know death. We were created that the earth might be made sensible of her inhuman taste.

Djuna Barnes

When I die, my epitaph should read: She Paid the Bills. That's the story of my private life.

Gloria Swanson

RIP

Lady Dolly cried terribly for a fortnight, and thought she cried for love, when she only cried for worry. In another fortnight or so she had ceased to cry, had found out that crape brightened her pretty tea-rose skin.

Ouida

I am sorry the good Sannes is dead; it was a pleasure to see him play at piquet, as coldly and as dryly as if he had really been in his coffin.

Marie de Sévigné

Well, I only hope he saved some of my money to pay for his funeral.

Maria Callas on the death of her agent

He loves her as if she were dead.

Geraldine Endsor Jewsbury

How could they tell?
Dorothy Parker's reaction to the death of American president Calvin Coolidge

The type of man who will end up dying in his own arms.
Mamie van Doren on Warren Beatty

My grandmother was a very tough woman. She buried three husbands. Two of them were just napping.

Rita Rudner

So your husband is dead. Peace be with him. That's one less
menace in your life.

Colette

I cannot say with you that I personally much regret Rachel.
George Sand on the death of the actress Rachel Félix

I have missed Hélène Picard and her richly provincial
genius.

Colette

She's as strong as an ox. She'll be turned into Bovril when
she dies.

Margot Asquith on Lady Desborough

We hoped sudden death would befall the Keynes.
Virginia Woolf, referring to the economist
Maynard Keynes and his wife, Lydia Lopokova

That woman was never any more than a piece of scenery,
and now nothing remains.

Colette

Only think of Mrs Holder's being dead! Poor woman, she
has done the only thing in the world she could possibly do
to make one cease to abuse her.

Jane Austen

Mrs Marjoribanks … devoted all her powers, during the lastten years of her life, to the solacement and care of that poor self which other people neglected. The consequence was, that when she disappeared from her sofa — except for the mere physical fact that she was no longer there — no one, except her maid, whose occupation was gone, could have found out much difference.

Margaret Oliphant

Lady Jane was as nearly broken-hearted as so cold a woman could be. She had loved her husband better than anything in this life, except herself.

Mary Braddon

Poor old rotten egg Joan. I kept my mouth shut about her for nearly a quarter of a century, but she was a mean, tipsy, powerful, rotten-egg lady.

Mercedes McCambridge on Joan Crawford

God was very good to the world. He took her from us.

Bette Davis on Miriam Hopkins

Now she is dead she greets Christ with a nod, —
(He was a carpenter) — but she knows God.

Virginia McCormick

Index

Ace, Jane 152
Ada Cleveland (fictional character) 256
Aird, Catherine 177
Alcott, Louisa May 225
Alexander, Shana 82
Allen, Gracie 202
Allen, Maria 184
Alther, Lisa 115, 166
Amos, Tori 158, 159
Anderson, Pamela 216
Andrews, Julie 137, 138, 145
Anger, Jane 9
Anne, Princess 176, 213, 214
Annesley, Maude 281
Anonymous quotes 15, 20, 28, 71, 117, 241
Anthony, Susan B. 229
Antrimz, Minna 55
Arnim, Elizabeth von vii, 292
Arnold, Sue 85, 99
Arnould, Sophie 87, 161, 163, 259
Asquith, Margot 2, 110, 128, 175, 272, 303
Astell, Mary 11
Astor, Mary 138
Astor, Nancy 29, 71, 220
Atherton, Gertrude 13, 39, 94, 114, 128, 131, 187, 207, 213, 226, 232, 233, 274, 275, 278, 279, 281, 282, 284, 294, 296
Atwood, Margaret 7, 43, 46, 125
Austen, Jane 12, 70, 82, 97, 107, 110, 120, 123, 232, 257, 296, 304

Bachi, Madame 177
Baddeley, Hermione 146
Bagnold, Enid 11, 54, 61, 147, 158, 160, 254, 269, 299
Baker, Belle 160
Ball, Lucille 218
Bankhead, Tallulah 45, 61, 62, 75, 111, 121, 128, 131, 134, 136, 138, 140, 141, 171, 192, 193, 232, 235, 256, 276
Bara, Theda 149
Barcynska, Countess 10
Bardot, Brigitte 17, 147
Barnes, Djuna 42, 43, 184, 221, 249, 288, 298, 299, 300, 301
Barr, Roseanne 14, 51
Barrymore, Ethel 138
Bashkirtseff, Marie 6, 45
Bautzer, Greg 140
Baylis, Lilian 108
Beard, Miriam 15, 245
Beatty, Warren 302
Beaumenard, Mlle de 161
Behar, Joy 87, 293
Bell, Vanessa 172, 295
Bennett, Constance 102, 217
Bernhardt, Sarah 148, 162, 180
Bernstein, Aline 184
Best, Mollie 199
Bibesco, Elizabeth 301
Bird, Caroline 37
Blessington, Marguerite 69, 279
Bloom, Amy 128
Bombeck, Erma 79, 93,

95, 96, 100, 101, 204, 206, 262, 295
Bow, Clara 119, 144, 145, 146
Bowles, Caroline 119
Bracken, Peg 3, 9, 31, 107, 172, 193, 201, 222, 223, 224, 241, 290, 292
Braddon, Mary 25, 31, 51, 71, 112, 124, 126, 194, 207, 224, 226, 304
Bradstreet, Anne 255
Branch, James Cavell 258
Brand, Jo 97, 101, 157, 180, 198, 200, 218, 221, 246, 247
Brando, Marlon 144
Brayfield, Celia 175, 249
Brent, Evelyn 144
Brice, Fanny 50, 63, 135, 176, 191, 215
Brittain, Vera 247
Brontë, Charlotte 4, 10, 47, 108, 112, 285, 288, 295
Brontë sisters 120
Brooks, Louise 118, 140, 143, 144, 145
Brougham, Lord 26
Broughton, Rhoda 32, 51, 52, 72, 96, 103, 110, 126, 128, 154, 159, 184, 193, 225, 226
Brown, Helen Gurley 18, 22, 23, 42, 47, 50, 51, 60, 64, 106, 156, 160, 198, 204, 223, 240, 241, 290
Brown, Mel 148
Brown, Rita Mae 46, 88, 89, 166, 174, 190, 221,

Index

263, 299, 300
Browning, Elizabeth
    Barrett 256
Budd, Zola 268
Bull, Mary 229
Bunton, Emma 228
Burchill, Julie 19, 20, 22,
    32, 35, 42, 52, 53, 60,
    62, 64, 65, 68, 74, 92,
    100, 137, 191, 211, 238,
    241, 248, 253, 255, 291,
    293
Burney, Fanny 82, 153,
    296
Buron, Nicole de 64, 192
Butler, Samuel 8
Byrne, Julia Clara 192,
    205, 231, 257

Calamity Jane 178
Callas, Maria 106, 147,
    185, 239, 267, 302
Calogeropoulos, Lisa 229
Campbell, Mrs Patrick
    111, 129
Canova, Judy 198
Carlyle, Jane 79
Carlyle, Thomas 79
Carter, Elizabeth 73, 173
Cartland, Barbara 63, 157
Cary, Joyce 187, 258
Cather, Willa 18
Cavendish, Margaret,
    Duchess of Newcastle
    149
Centlivre, Susannah 194
Chanel, Coco 11, 119,
    173, 220, 223, 239
Chanel, Gabrielle 20,
    185, 227, 244
Chaplin, Charlie 26
Cher 6, 49, 68, 77, 94,
    149, 243, 247
Chesler, Phyllis 210, 211
Chester, Laura 10, 36,
    100, 157
Choiseul, Louise

Honorine de 47
Cholmondeley, Mary
    106
Christie, Agatha 44, 83,
    202
Christie, Amanda 183
Churchill, Jennie Jerome
    29, 84
Churchill, Winston 236,
    248, 259
Cleghorn, Ellen 183
Cleveland, Ava 120, 216
Clifford, Mrs W. K. 43,
    172
Clift, Montgomery 143
Clinton, Hillary
    Rodham 73, 85, 99,
    148, 156, 183, 231
Clinton, Kate 7
Coke, Lady Mary 180
Colbert, Claudette 138
Cole, Nina 208
Colet, Louise 38, 39, 43,
    44, 233
Colette 17, 37, 65, 83,
    119, 153, 177, 182, 196,
    199, 210, 227, 267, 303
Collier, Jane 46
Columbus, Christopher
    272
Connelly, Mary Frances
    170
Conquest, Joan 62
Coolidge, Calvin 302
Cooper, Gary 144
Cooper, Jilly 263
Cope, Wendy 6, 8, 115
Corelli, Marie 70
Coward, Noel 131
Cowl, Jane 232
Craigie, Pearl May Teresa
    7
Craik, Dinah 93
Crawford, Joan 138, 139,
    175, 233, 304
Crewe, Lady 187
Croce, Arlene 26

Cruse, Heloise 85
Cunnington, Phyllis 234
Curtis, Tony 143

Daly, Mary 35
Darling, Julia 94, 199, 243
Davis, Bette vii, 17, 37,
    50, 87, 129, 131, 135,
    136, 138, 139, 142, 143,
    145, 146, 149, 162, 170,
    233, 299, 304
Davis, Elizabeth Gould 7
Davis, Joan 242
Davys, Mary 255
Day, Laraine 137
Day, Lillian 75
De Wolfe, Elsie 130
De Wolfe Hopper 130
Dean, Carl 77
Delaney, Mrs 118
Delaney, Shelagh 277
Deneuve, Catherine 147
Desborough, Lady 303
Lady Georgiana Spencer
    205, 248
Dewar, Isla 175, 190, 236,
    244
Dewey, Thomas 24
Dickinson, Emily 178,
    294
Dietrich, Marlene 38, 42,
    45, 72, 118, 134, 135,
    142, 143, 149, 164, 232,
    242, 244, 283, 291, 292,
    300
Diller, Phyllis 25, 97, 206,
    219, 220, 238
Dix, Dorothy 42, 77, 78,
    85, 93, 211, 242
Dixon, Ella Hepworth
    80, 185
Dohm, Hedwig 36
Donelly, Tanya 212
Dors, Dolly 28
Douglas, Mrs Fanny 11,
    72, 301
Dressler, Marie 53, 98,

Index

141, 148, 160, 190, 210, 213, 238, 266, 269
Duffey, Mrs E. B. 117
Dunbar, Helen 145
Duncan, Isadora 68, 88
Dunn, Mary 83, 92, 181, 226
Dykestra, Lillian K. 24

Eclair, Jenny 23, 49, 50, 59, 62, 74, 92, 93, 97, 100, 102, 164, 173, 174, 196, 201, 202, 205, 266, 267, 268, 269, 292
Eden, The Honorable Emily 123, 211, 212, 230, 231, 236
Ehrenreich, Barbara 124
Ekland, Britt 167
Eliot, George 18, 72, 186, 233, 252, 257, 299
Elizabeth II, queen of England 130, 202, 213, 279, 291
Elizabeth (Queen Mother) 128, 202
Ellerbee, Linda 234
Elliot, Mama Cass 174
Ellis, Alice Thomas 44, 54, 74, 81, 86, 107, 176, 201, 203, 243, 253, 267, 280
Ellmann, Lucy 8, 10, 14, 16, 21, 37, 86, 101, 139, 278, 283
Ephron, Nora 17, 32, 33, 43, 48, 81, 86, 155, 211, 258, 293
Eyting, Rose 131

Fahey, Siobhan 170
Fairbanks, Doug 144
Falkender, Marcia 245
"Fang" (stage character) 25, 97
Farmer, Frances 138
Farr, Florence 86

Farrow, Mia 143, 217
Faulks, Sebastian 257
Félix, Rachel 73, 303
Ferber, Edna 48, 92, 99, 207, 212, 218, 227, 238, 240
Ferguson, Rachel vii, 116, 125, 145, 193, 221, 249, 252, 259
Ferguson, Sheila 63
Fern, Fanny 9, 69, 79, 80, 81, 82, 98, 120, 121, 174, 256, 283
Ferrier, Susan 25, 122, 123
Fields, Totie 205, 206
Fields, W.C. 148
Finch, Anne, Countess of Winchelsea 28
Fini, Leonor 230
Fisher, Carrie 65, 174, 245, 290
Fisher, M. E. K. 284
Fleming, Ian 154
Flynn, Errol 143
Forrest, Emma 218, 228
Foster, Augustus Clifford 124
Foster, Lady Elizabeth 179, 187
Fowler, Ellen T. 76, 213
Fox, Della 132
Franklin, Irene 158
Franklin, Miles 47
Fraser, Lady Antonia 229
French, Dawn 22, 280
French, Marilyn 17, 35, 36
Freud, Sigmund 25, 26, 58
Friedan, Betty 2, 58, 87, 245
Friganza, Trixie 206
Fry, Roger 295
Fuller, Margaret 111, 132, 295

Gable, Clark 136
Gabor, Zsa Zsa 70, 84, 88, 96, 136, 140, 160, 194, 220
Gandhi, Indira 243
Garbo, Greta 141, 149
Garden, Mary 45
Gardner, Ava 71, 129, 143, 145
Garland, Judy 136, 147
Garson, Greer 144
Gaskell, Mrs 111, 200, 227, 253
Gates, Georgina Stickland 267
Gaynor, Mitzi 74
Genĺt 16, 248, 284
Genghis Kahn 247
George, Phyllis 250
Gerster, Etelka 131
Gilbert, Jack 149
Gilman, Charlotte Perkins 76, 92, 201, 204, 272
Gilot, Françoise 149
Gingold, Hermione vii, 93, 132, 195, 200
Glaser, Sherry 97
Glyn, Elinor 3, 12, 44, 55, 71, 72, 77, 98, 109, 120, 152, 171, 193, 216, 256
Goddard, Paulette 195
Goodman, Emily Jane 210, 211
Gordon, Ruth 300
Gournay, Marie de 15
Gower, Lady Harriet Leveson 124, 179
Graffiti 8, 20, 21, 34, 88
Grafton, Sue 262
Graham, Virginia 262
Grainger, Stewart 144
Grand, Elspeth 144
Grand, Sarah 10
Grant, Cary 138
Grant, Ruth W. 171
Gray, Effie 111

Index

Greeley, Mrs 132
Greenwood, Charlotte 266
Greer, Germaine 16, 22, 24, 30, 31, 63, 73, 75, 94, 118, 155, 156, 164, 166, 186, 222, 244, 245, 267, 268, 276, 286, 299
Grenfell, Joyce 240
Greville, Ronald 111
Gryneston, Elizabeth 212
Gudmundsdottir, Bj`rk 58, 275
Guiccioli, Countess Teresa 205
Guimard, Mlle 259

Haber, Joyce 145
Hadden, Belinda 183
Hall, Jerry 85
Hall, Margaret 282
Halliday, Toni 16
Halsey, Margaret 192, 199, 202, 276, 280, 281, 288
Hamilton, David Diddy 24
Hamilton, Jane 117, 216, 235
Hamilton, Lady Emma 111
Harlow, Jean 128, 142
Harper, Ida Husted 119
Harriet, Lady Ashburton 15
Harris, Mildred 140
Harry, Debbie 106, 219
Harvey, Laurence 146
Hawes, Elizabeth 7, 59, 78, 92, 96, 106, 107, 114, 120, 199, 215, 224, 257
Hawkins, Laetitia Matilda 114, 116
Hawthorne, Sophia 208
Hayes, Helen 12, 95, 147, 239, 298

Hayworth, Rita 2, 73, 118, 148
Heide, Wilma Scott 241
Heidi Abromowitz (fictional character) 160, 162, 170, 207
Heimel, Cynthia 13, 19, 21, 23, 63, 88, 156, 173, 186, 225, 276
Hellman, Lillian 124, 141, 177, 187
Henry VIII, king of England 180
Hepburn, Katharine 35, 52, 135, 144, 185, 238
Hilts, Elizabeth 64, 176
Hitler, Adolf 248
Hogg, Elizabeth 263
Holland, Lady 205
Hollander, Xaviera 253
Hopkins, Miriam 304
Hopper, Edna Wallace 89
Hopper, Hedda 26, 49, 89, 134, 136, 138, 141, 142, 143, 144, 175, 195, 232, 236, 249
Howars, Barbara 33, 239, 246, 291
Hudson, Rock 135
Hughes, Howard 140
Hurst, Fannie 48, 195
Hurston, Zora Neale 49

Inchbald, Elizabeth 277

Jaeger, Lena 195
Jaffe, Rona 46, 47, 55, 165, 198, 272
Jefferson, Mr 273
Jett, Joan 216
Jewsbury, Geraldine Endsor 44, 75, 126, 172, 231, 302
John Gaunt (fictional character) 256
Johnstone, Augusta 78, 252

Jones, Grace 37
Jones, Mary "Mother" 12, 184
Jones, Rickie Lee 175
Jong, Erica 22, 23, 32, 50, 54, 55, 58, 59, 60, 69, 98, 157, 178, 255
Joplin, Janis 300
Jouvenel, Henry de 153
Judd, Naomi 171

Kael, Pauline 137, 138
Kahn, Alice 28, 63, 65, 76, 147, 252, 253, 254, 290
Kallen, Lucille 38, 78, 79, 80
Kendal, Dame Margaret 162
Kennedy, Florynce R. 94, 165, 241
Kent, Princess Michael of 191, 268
Keppel, Alice 111
Keppel, Violet 29
Kerr, Deborah 56
Kerr, Jean 13, 15, 69, 99, 100, 102, 210, 212, 214, 215
Keynes, Maynard 303
King, Florence 106
Kizer, Carolyn 235
Knight, India 51, 87, 115, 118, 217
Kreps, Juanita 9
Kuslansky, Laurie 291

La Fayette, Marie de 18
Lamarr, Hedy 13, 29, 65, 135, 146, 165, 202, 284
Lamartine, Alphonse de 254
Lamb, Lady Caroline 82, 83, 96, 114, 178, 181, 236
Lanchester, Elsa 145
lang, k. d. 23, 30, 46, 148,

293
Langtry, Lily 145
Latour, Thérèse L 231
Laughton, Charles 235
Lawrence, D. H. 110, 256
Lawrence, Margaret 120
Lawrenson, Helen 145
Lear, Amanda 179
Lebowitz, Fran 50, 60,
    101, 115, 198, 199, 252,
    276, 292, 300
Lederer, Helen 184
Lee, Gypsy Rose 163,
    183
Lee-Potter, Linda 242
Lehman, Rosamund 154
Leifer, Carol 180
Leigh, Vivien 280
Lenclos, Ninon de 25,
    163
lesbian author 32
Leslie, Eliza 194
Lette, Kathy 2, 23, 45, 75,
    78, 88, 92, 97, 101, 157,
    163, 165, 167, 173, 182,
    200, 213, 220
Lewes, George 186
Lieven, Princess de 231
Lillie, Beatrice 132, 203,
    215, 219, 259, 272
Lilly, Doris 39, 158, 193,
    286, 287
Lipman, Maureen 98,
    101, 137, 172, 200, 217,
    218, 239, 243, 257, 292
Little, Mary Wilson 46
Lloyd-George, David
    175
Long, Renee 114, 215
Longsworth, Alice
    Roosevelt 109
Loos, Anita 19, 33, 55, 58,
    119, 139, 140, 164, 195,
    196, 203, 257, 285
Lopokova, Lydia 118,
    303
Loren, Sophia 61

Lorimer, Norma 52, 77,
    195, 286, 287
Love, Courtney 94, 99,
    170, 179, 183, 190, 293
Lovric, Michelle 10
Lowell, Amy 125
Luce, Clare Boothe 30,
    34, 129, 131, 141, 247
LuPone, Patti 48
Lynn, Loretta 173

Mabley, Jackie "Moms"
    21, 202, 233, 242, 299
Macaulay, Rose 120, 219,
    267
McCambridge,
    Mercedes 304
McCarthy, Laura Flynn
    198
McCarthy, Mary 187,
    253, 284
McCormick, Virginia
    262, 304
McGinley, Phyllis 19
MacLaine, Shirley 34
Madonna 34, 38, 61, 62,
    137, 146, 161, 162, 165,
    170, 232, 239, 240, 259
Maintenon, Madame de
    114
Mansfield, Jayne 142, 154
Mansfield, Katherine 53,
    71, 86, 124, 167, 200,
    217, 219, 259
Margaret, Princess 174,
    291
Margolis, Sue 201, 204,
    298
Marker, Pat 32
Marlborough, Duchess of
    111
Marston, Mrs 254
Martha the Fainthearted
    Feminist (fictional
    character) 38, 49, 244
Martin, Andrea 17
Martineau, Harriet 26,

33-4, 34, 69, 255, 277
Mathews, Anne 13, 14,
    15, 130, 173, 191
Maxwell, Elsa 182, 194,
    223, 278
Mead, Margaret 9
Mel C 275
Melba Toast (fictional
    character) 165
Melbourne, Lady
    Elizabeth 109
Merchant, Vivien 229
Meynell, Alice 182, 278
Midler, Bette 214, 242,
    246, 274, 279
Millay, Edna St Vincent
    238
Miller, Arthur 139
Milne, A. A. 126
Miss Piggy (Muppet) 204
Mitford, Mary Russell
    122, 123, 284
Mitford, Nancy 280
Monroe, Marilyn 58, 65,
    99, 139, 140, 143, 149,
    171, 181, 217, 222, 245
Montagu, Elizabeth 4
Montagu, Lady Mary
    Wortley 24, 54, 69, 111,
    112, 166, 176, 180, 181,
    235, 280, 285, 294
Montaran, Madame de
    212
Moodie, Susanna 84
Moore, Doris Langley 2,
    3
Moore, Jane 13, 228
Moore, John 245
Moore, Lorrie 7, 20, 43,
    50, 52, 53, 54, 55, 60,
    79, 191, 210
Moore, Suzanne 216
More, Hannah 119, 120
Morgan, Robin 154
Morley, Eric 24
Morrell, Lady Ottoline
    14, 109, 110, 175, 256,

Index

272
Morris, Jan 286
Movie Talk 129
Mumford, Ethel Watts
92, 134, 185, 190, 248,
298
Murphy, Maureen 246
Murray, Judith Sargent 19

Naldi, Nita 142
Nelson, Mariah Burton
246, 262
Nevill, Lady Dorothy
235
Nichols, Diane 3, 21
Normand, Mabel 187
Norris, Kathleen 87
Norton, The Hon. Mrs
155

Oberon, Merle 146
O'Brien , Edna 39
O'Donnell, Rosie 263
O'Hara, Maureen 145
Oliphant, Margaret 296,
304
Olivier, Laurence 143
Onassis, Aristotle 229
Onassis, Jackie 165, 229
Ouida 16, 31, 42, 45, 52,
73, 106, 108, 115, 124,
152, 153, 166, 171, 174,
186, 206, 224, 225, 226,
238, 240, 244, 268, 269,
287, 296, 298, 299, 302

Palmerston, Lady 111
Pankhurst, Christabel 36
Pankhurst, Sylvia 248
Pardo Baz·n, Emilia 9
Parker, Dorothy 2, 56,
110, 114, 115, 116, 125,
126, 128, 129, 131, 134,
135, 142, 160, 162, 176,
180, 187, 225, 232, 254,
256, 258, 266, 292, 298,
301, 302

Parsons, Louella 136
Parton, Dolly 28, 42, 58,
61, 64, 77, 102, 124,
154, 155, 159, 161, 203,
214, 216, 217, 218, 221,
228, 234, 250, 291
Parturier, Françoise 22,
117
Paterson, Isabel 238, 253
Patti, Adelina 131
Pearl, Minnie 196
Perkins, Charlotte 86
Phillips, Melanie 6, 162
Piaf, Edith 116
Picard, Hélène 303
Pickford, Mary 146, 187
Piercy, Marge 37, 80
Pinard, Mlle 181
Pinter, Harold 229
Pisan, Christine de 4
Platis, Madame
Merveilleux du 122
Plutarch 29
Pogrebin, Letty Cottin
17, 240
Pompadour, Madame de
275
Pope, Alexander 181
Post, Emily 301
Pound, Ezra 125
Prager, Emily 203
Proulx, Annie 6, 263
Puisieux, Madame de
106

Quentin, Caroline 205

Raeburn, Anna 137
Rawlings, Marjorie,
Kinnan 53
Reagan, Nancy 124
Reddin of Undern 24
Redford, Robert 25
Renoir, Pierre Auguste
259
Retton, Mary Lou 175
Riding, Laura 120, 275

Rieux, Madame de 182
Ritter, Erika 7
Ritter, Thelma 145
Rivers, Joan 18, 46, 65,
74, 79, 83, 89, 93, 139,
152, 160, 162, 165, 170,
196, 203, 206, 207, 215,
219, 228, 232, 263, 300
Robertson, Nan 33
Ronstadt, Linda 159
Rook, Jean 24, 61, 135,
136, 163, 176, 179, 185,
214, 262
Rothschild, Baroness
Guy de 194
Rowland, Helen 6, 8, 11,
14, 19, 20, 29, 30, 31,
32, 36, 43, 49, 50, 51,
68, 70, 72, 74, 76, 80,
81, 83, 84, 85, 89, 95,
152, 153, 154, 155, 156,
157, 158, 170, 171, 184,
211, 233, 234
Rubinstein, Helena 210,
216
Ruckelshaus, Jill 33
Rudner, Rita 9, 11, 18,
38, 69, 70, 72, 73, 157,
196, 262, 302
Rumanian proverb 76
Ruskin, Effie 229
Russell, Lillian 76

Sagan, Françoise 45
St John, Adela Rogers 25,
79, 146
Salkind, Betsy 28
Sanborn, Kate vii, 120,
257
Sand, George 29, 39, 82,
116, 214, 221, 254, 295,
300, 303
Saunders, Jennifer 280
Sayers, Dorothy L. 190
Schaffer, Zenna 262
Schiaparelli, Elsa 15, 19,
33, 186, 201, 210, 227,

Conspicuous
Consumption

Conspicuous Consumption

I've found that too much of a good thing can be wonderful.
Mae West

What's so fucking bad about getting what you want?
Courtney Love

There were three little words that ruled Eileen's life — it's not enough. "It's not enough," she would cry, looking desperately round.
Isla Dewar

To have a beautiful wife and not surround her with beautiful things isn't as bad as castration, but it runs a close second.
Rita Mae Brown

The keeping of an idle woman is a badge of superior social status.
Dorothy L. Sayers

In the midst of life we are in debt.
Ethel Watts Mumford

WEALTH

Think what stupid things the people must have done with their money who say they're "happier without"!
Edith Wharton

I'm told a pawnbroker won't give you half as much on your silver if it's crested.
Marie Dressler

Conspicuous Consumption

I'm overdrawn at the bank. I won't say how much, but if you saw it written down, you'd think it was a sex chatline number.

Julie Burchill

I've been poor and I've been rich. Rich is better.

Fanny Brice

Our phone bill is equivalent to the national debt of Vanuatu.

Isabel Wolff

Yuppies, we knew, were greedy, shallow and small ... We renamed the seven dwarves: Artsy, Fartsy, Cranky, Sleazy, Beasty, Dud and Yuppie.

Lorrie Moore

£70,000? I couldn't begin to live on that.

Princess Michael of Kent

A gold rush is what happens when a line of chorus girls spot a man with a bank roll.

Mae West

He who buys what he does not want, will soon want what he cannot buy.

Anne Mathews

I live way below my means.

Oprah Winfrey

FOOD & DRINK

It has long been my boast that I can read or eat anything.
Katharine Whitehorn

These restaurant people really have a talent for charging
exorbitant prices for the things I like best.
Nicole de Buron

But even when the wolf was at the door, the butter on her
breakfast-table had to be trimmed with rose-buds.
Julia Clara Byrne on Madame Vestris

[English women] run off their dinners with a satin-smooth
suavity which makes American hostesses look like victims of
St Vitus' dance.
Margaret Halsey

People who eat white bread have no dreams.
Diana Vreeland

Are the rich the new poor with their horrible mucked-
about food, where nothing is allowed to look or taste of
itself?
Sue Townsend

Frankly, I have contributed a great deal to the carousing
phase of my legend.
Tallulah Bankhead

You've heard, I'm sure, about Tallulah the toper! Tallulah the tosspot! Tallulah, the gal who gets tight as a tick! Let's face it, my dears, I have been tight as a tick! Fried as a mink! Stiff as a goat!

Tallulah Bankhead

It is not easy to get an American girl drunk, and many men have passed out trying.

Doris Lilly

You are not as bright as you feel, after the second drink.

Peg Bracken

It could not be denied that Miss Cleveland was as attractive a modern young woman as ever drank three cocktails before dinner, and a bottle of champagne all to herself at the repast.

Elinor Glyn

These days, champagne gives me a sensation as of one treading on sponges; ale finds out my liver, and, renewing old acquaintance, discovers incompatibility, ending in recrimination and scenes.

Rachel Ferguson

Whether it was all love and no champagne, or all champagne and no love, or half love and half champagne, or three quarters love and one quarter champagne, or one quarter love and three quarters champagne, I cannot say; but certain it is that Hugh be inconveniently tender.

Rhoda Broughton

I've had my allotment of liquor — and probably twenty other people's.

Grace Slick

I mean, alcohol in excess can cause untold misery, not to mention the bother of humping the empties.

Victoria Wood

PARTIES

The best parties are given by people who cannot afford them.

Elsa Maxwell

Avoid giving invitations to bores — they will come without.

Eliza Leslie

Sixteen hundred people are just too many.

Baroness Guy de Rothschild, describing a party at her château

JEWELS

"Not another diamond bracelet, I hope," she said, with a touch of petulance.

Mary Braddon

Nothing melts a Woman's Heart like gold.

Susannah Centlivre

I never hated a man enough to give him his diamonds back.

Zsa Zsa Gabor

Conspicuous Consumption

Paulette's a natural-born collector. When she was fourteen her mother told her it was bad luck to buy jewellery for herself, and she promised to mind her mother.

Hedda Hopper on Paulette Goddard

Mother says never accept statues from strange men, only jewellery.

Hermione Gingold

I have always felt a gift diamond shines better than one you buy for yourself.

Mae West

SHOPPING

I always say it doesn't pay to economize. It's the extravagant women who are most respected by their husbands.

Fannie Hurst

There are dress-drunkards …

Norma Lorimer

I do not like to take gentlemen shopping for small size nicknacks and give them a false sense of values.

Anita Loos

It is a sad woman who buys her own perfume.

Lena Jaeger

Conspicuous Consumption

Men like cars, women like clothes. Women only like cars because they take them to the clothes.

Rita Rudner

If I am wild about a dress, I buy one for now and another to put away so I will still look nice when my career has come to an end.

Joan Rivers

And I always seem to think that the most delightful part of a shopping tour is to frequintly change your mind.

Anita Loos

I have very often deprived myself of the necessities of life, but I have never consented to give up a luxury.

Colette

The upper-middle classes are never satisfied — they always take things back to shops and demand to have the sales assistant beaten.

Jenny Eclair

The price tag on my hat seems to be symbolic of all human frailty.

Minnie Pearl

Food, Fat &
Dieting

I like anything that comes under the heading, "It's got calories and you can put it in your mouth".

Jo Brand

I'm still looking for a man who could excite me as much as a baked potato.

Laura Flynn McCarthy

I have food dreams instead of sex dreams.

Rona Jaffe

If I had to choose between sex and food, I would choose food, but I'd choose sex over nearly everything else.

Helen Gurley Brown

If food did not exist it would be well-nigh impossible to get certain types off the phone, as one would be unable to say, "Look, I've got to run but let's have dinner sometime soon".

Fran Lebowitz

When I found out we are what we eat, I stopped eatin' pig cracklins and sow belly.

Judy Canova

Food is welcome at both meal and snack time. It goes well with most any beverage and by and large makes the best sandwich.

Fran Lebowitz

Anyway, food is a very important thing and perhaps the most important thing about it for you is never to cook food that a man can understand.

Elizabeth Hawes

If I had a son of marriageable age, I should say to him: "Beware of young women who love neither wine nor truffles nor cheese nor music."

Colette

Beware of the man who loves his mother's macaroni and cheese more than he loves sex. Or you. Or anything.

Linda Stasi

There are more ways of killing a man than choking him to death with butter.

Mollie Best

Ask your child what he wants for dinner only if he's buying.

Fran Lebowitz

Lunch was more interesting than history.

Julia Darling

BAD FOOD

The soup, thin and dark and utterly savourless, tasted as if it had been drained out of the umbrella stand.

Margaret Halsey on English food

Last night I dined at a Russian house, a real Russian dinner. First soup made of mutton, and sour kraut; very nasty and horrible to smell … Then *rôti* of some common sort; then *gelinottes* of Russian partridge, which feed on the young sprouts of the pine trees, and taste strong of turpentine.

Mrs Gaskell

And the food. It's got no nerves. You know what I mean? It seems to lie down and wait for you; the very steaks are meek. There's no contact between you and it. You're not attracted… As to the *purée de pommes de terre* you feel inclined to call it "uncle".

Katherine Mansfield

[In his fridge] I found yogurt whose expiry date read "When Dinosaurs Roamed the Earth".

Kathy Lette

In Jewish restaurants the waiter is always right.

Maureen Lipman

Cultured pearls are formed by artificially irritating the oyster by various means. Such as whispering to it as it lies cosily in bed: "Don't look now, but there's an R in the month."

Hermione Gingold

The name Big Mac is generally supposed to have come about because it is a big McDonald's burger, but in fact it was named after a big raincoat whose taste it so closely resembles.

Jo Brand

Naomi ordered achiote and honey-cured elk *carpaccio* with *chorizo*, pomegranates, green lentil horseradish mash and *miso wasable* syrup.

Sue Margolis

The anchovy starter was the worst thing I've eaten since I inadvertently swallowed a large flying insect while laughing open-mouthed in Greece.

Sue Townsend

COOKING

The long-suffering human system (perhaps toughened by ages of home-cooking) will adapt itself even to slow death.

Charlotte Perkins Gilman

A good cook is like a sorceress who dispenses happiness.

Elsa Schiaparelli

I can't see the point in making tons of food if people are just going to sit there and eat it.

Jenny Eclair

Don't take any recipe on faith. There are some hostile recipes in this world.

Peg Bracken

Just as every human being believes he has a novel in him, so every uxorious husband believes his wife has a cookery book in her.

Alice Thomas Ellis

When the little roast burns, the big one is done.
American radio comedienne Gracie Allen's method of cooking meat,
by putting two joints in the oven at the same time

DRINK

A lot of men get very funny about women drinking: they
don't really like it. Well, I'm sorry lads, but if we didn't get
pissed, most of you would never get a shag.

Jenny Eclair

You teach 'em Mother Hubbard went to the cupboard to
get her poor dog a bone. I say Mother Hubbard had gin in
that cupboard.

Jackie "Moms" Mabley

I never liked beer. It's plebeian. It goes with dirty undershirts.

Hedy Lamarr

When the Queen asked for a glass of wine at lunch, the
Queen-Mother reportedly asked her: "Is that wise? You
know you have to reign all afternoon."

from The Wit and Wisdom of the Royal Family

Coffee in England always tastes like a chemistry experiment.

Agatha Christie

English coffee tastes the way a long-standing family joke
sounds, when you try to explain it to outsiders.

Margaret Halsey

I can never take for granted the euphoria produced by a cup of coffee. I'm grateful every day that it isn't banned as a drug.

Anita Loos

Eat drink and be merry, for tomorrow we diet.

Alice Thomas Ellis

DIETARY CONSIDERATIONS

I do not overeat because my mother slapped me when I was five. I overeat because I'm a damned hog.

Dolly Parton

By six years of age I was a fatso who finished her midnight snack just in time for breakfast.

Joan Rivers

I used to fear that ice cream would be the ruin of me, but I gave up giving it up a long time ago.

Beatrice Lillie

I felt as though everything I ate went instantly to my thighs — like a squirrel storing food in its cheeks.

Joan Rivers

Binge-eating was clearly an early female Neanderthal survival trait to ensure women got enough to eat.

Emily Prager

Food, Fat & Dieting

Misery makes some people deep.
It always makes me wide.

Judith Viorst

DIETING

Never eat more than you can lift.

Miss Piggy

I have dieted continuously for the last two decades and lost a total of seven hundred and fifty-eight pounds. By all calculations, I should be hanging from a charm bracelet.

Erma Bombeck

Terror is the word for facing a day with only eight hundred calories — black ugly terror.

Helen Gurley Brown

I've lost the same half-stone so many times my cellulite's got déjà vu … I don't need a diet. What I need is a tapeworm.

Sue Margolis

A diet cookie has one hundred cals, and who wants just one cookie?

Helen Gurley Brown

Ghosts have been seen and believed in from the earliest days of gluttony and indigestion.

Charlotte Perkins Gilman

Food, Fat and Dieting

Why go to the gym when you can relax unconscious under a skilled surgeon's knife?

Jenny Eclair

LOOKING FAT

I've got my figure back after giving birth. Sad, I'd hoped to get somebody else's.

Caroline Quentin

Miss Van Osburgh was a large girl with flat surfaces and no high lights: Jack Stepney had once said of her that she was as reliable as roast mutton.

Edith Wharton

I break all the rules and wear everything. Ruffles, ostrich feathers, fox coats. You look fat in fox anyway, so if you start fat, you only look a little fatter.

Plump American comedienne Totie Fields

Her figure is corpulent, her complexion coarse, one eye gone, and her neck immense.

Lady Holland, describing Lady Georgiana Spencer

One of these gentlemen assured me that her complexion reminded him of ... boiled pork(!) ... she had the appearance of a short bolster with a string around its middle. Worse than this, it seems that the Guiccioli waddled like a duck.

Julia Clara Byrne on Countess Teresa Guiccioli,
Byron's last mistress

If the Venus de Medici could be animated into life, women would only remark that her waist was large.

Ouida

When I started in show business I was thin enough to be blown through a keyhole. Now I can't even get through the door.

Trixie Friganza

I kept trying to walk in sideways, because you can suck in your stomach, but I defy anybody to suck in hips.

Joan Rivers

I'll come right out and say I'm fat. I think I'm precious at this weight.

Plump American comedienne Totie Field's way of coping with hecklers

I'm a loser. When I grew my own bustle, they went out of style.

Erma Bombeck

There was a time when I had a twenty-three inch waist. I was ten years old at the time. As I recall, my measurements were 23-23-23.

Erma Bombeck

I don't know what her measurements are. We haven't had her surveyed yet.

Phyllis Diller on her stage mother-in-law, "Moby Dick"

In a sweater she looked like a walking dairy state.
Joan Rivers on her fictional character, Heidi Abromowitz

The pretty little women with eighteen-inch waists opined
that Miss Tempest was too big.
"She's very handsome, you know, and all that," they said
deprecatingly, "and her figure is quite splendid; but she's on
such a very large scale."

Mary Braddon

A fat girl with a fat girl's soul is a comedy. But a fat girl with
a thin girl's soul is a tragedy.

Edna Ferber

Of course, Lotta is rather drowsy now, but then she is grown
very fat; like a large chest of drawers covered in a black velvet
pall.

Virginia Woolf

She was a short woman, with a still beautiful figure above the
waist; it was growing massive below.

Gertrude Atherton

Hester bobbed up again as usual, grown fat and blowsy with
ankles like the thick end of asparagus.

Virginia Woolf

There was a great Duchess there, the Duchess of Palmella; and she is as big as a centre-table, and her features, in the midst of an acre of cheeks and chin, look as if they had lost themselves on a vast plain. Her arm is as large as Aunt Sue's waist, and her waist could not be measured very well. Though so huge and really monstrous, this poor lady is very young, — only twenty-four, — while I thought she was sixty. …I hope you will excuse that ugly blot on the paper. I do not at all know how it came there, — it seems to have something to do with the blotted life of the poor Duchess of Palmella. I am sure she will be glad when her soul soars out of its vast and misshapen house of clay.

Sophia Hawthorne

The Duchess de Mazarin had grown so very stout that it took ages to do up her corsets. A visitor coming to see her one day while she was being laced, one of her women ran to the door and cried out: "Don't come in till we've arranged the rolls of flesh!" I remember that this excessive plumpness aroused the admiration of the Turkish Ambassadors.

Elisabeth Louise Vigée-Le Brun

The word "jammed" described everything about her. She looked as if she had been shut up in a door once, and forgotten, and never let out till her whole appearance had gained its present squeezed look. Her head was squeezed, her face was squeezed, and her body was squeezed, and as to her clothes, they followed suit; her cap was squeezed, her bonnet was squeezed, and her dress was squeezed.

Nina Cole

Appearances

Appearances

Mirror, Mirror, On the Wall,
I Don't Want to Hear
One Word Out of You.

Jean Kerr

Remember — twenty per cent of women have inferiority
complexes. Seventy per cent have illusions.

Elsa Schiaparelli

I contend that every woman has the right to feel beautiful,
no matter how scrambled her features or how indifferent her
features.

Marie Dressler

I really believe that no woman is so devoid of charms that
she cannot make herself attractive along the lines of
whatever is most characteristically herself.

Helena Rubinstein

Women may feel like a million dollars when they look good
— but they haven't got a million dollars.

Phyllis Chesler and Emily Jane Goodman

The problem with a beautiful woman is that she makes
everyone around her feel hopelessly masculine.

Lorrie Moore

Too much courage has shone among female kind, and for
too many years, for women, under the pretext of loyalty, to
break the contract they signed with beauty.

Colette

Appearances

You know, it's always some American stick insect in a leotard with perfect legs and ears and so on that's there on the TV saying everyone is beautiful, we should learn to love ourselves as we are.

Helen Stevenson

Men who profess to worship beauty are generally content to adore it from a safe distance.

Dorothy Dix

Chic is beauty with all the sex, sweat and seed sucked out, the dry husk of lust.

Julie Burchill

As she had no hope of raising herself to the rank of a beauty, her only chance was bringing others down to her own level.

The Honourable Emily Eden

It is better to be dead than unkissable.

Helen Rowland

When a woman is described as having "lots of personality" — or a rich father — everyone knows that she is "ugly".

Phyllis Chesler and Emily Jane Goodman

If there is anything more boring to me than the problems of big-busted women, it is the problems of beautiful women.

Nora Ephron

A woman without beauty knows but half of life.

Madame de Montaran

It keeps me so busy being beautiful, and what the society writers call "well groomed," that I don't have time to sew the buttons on my underclothes.

Edna Ferber

I looked up at myself in the mirror, looking like something the cat hadn't even bothered to bring in.

Helen Stevenson

I feel I am rather sweet at dinner parties; let other women be trim and gorgeous.

Jean Kerr

People may go on talking for ever of the jealousies of pretty women; but for real genuine, hard-working envy there is nothing like an ugly woman with a taste for admiration. Her mortified vanity curdles into malevolence; and she calumniates where she cannot rival.

The Honourable Emily Eden

If women could learn to be as unattractive as men, it would go a long way towards demystifying females in bands.

Tanya Donelly

A fair woman is a paradise to the eye, a purgatory to the purse, and a hell to the soul.

Elizabeth Gryneston

Appearances

My experience is that the attractive women get the nice little things, and the unattractive ones the nice big things of this world.

Ellen T. Fowler

I loathe narcissism, but I approve of vanity.

Diana Vreeland

I can admire another woman's beauty with all the detachment of a Cook's tourist beholding the Coliseum by moonlight.

Marie Dressler

I am as fond of beauty spas as I am of being flayed alive with barbed wire.

Kathy Lette

It's a sign that self-image is negative and self-esteem is low when cosmetic surgery becomes just one more occasion for shame and thus for lying.

Gloria Steinem

If you are beautiful your husband is your slave, if you are plain, you are his upper servant.

Gertrude Atherton

FACE

It's most unfortunate that all my sons have such long eyelashes while my daughter hasn't any at all.

The Queen on Princess Anne

Appearances

Lipstick was the most fascinating thing to me because it was red and got the most attention. Also, it went on the mouth, which I figured was about the sexiest part of a woman that was all right to show in public.

Dolly Parton

Her face alone would make you ill.
George Sand, referring to one of her domestic staff

Princess Anne has teeth like dazzling tombstones.
Jean Rook

Such an attractive lass. So outdoorsy. She loves nature in spite of what it did to her.
Bette Midler on Princess Anne

You could not have said that I was "as cute as a speckled pup" without expecting the speckled pup to piss on your leg out of resentment.
Dolly Parton on her childhood freckles

I'm tired of all this nonsense about beauty being only skin deep. That's deep enough. What do you want — an adorable pancreas?
Jean Kerr

She is like a slug with a bleeding gash for a mouth.
Virginia Woolf on the artist Dorothy Todd

It's great to be laughed at, but just think, if only my nose had been a quarter of an inch shorter I could have been a femme fatale.

Beatrice Lillie

Get a clean, natural-line eyebrow by pulling out all your unnatural brows and pencilling in the natural ones.

Elizabeth Hawes

I do think a woman has supreme egotism who falls out of bed and faces the world with her face as is.

Renee Long

I fancy that only my nose went on growing after my twelfth birthday.

Beatrice Lillie

No woman on the stage today can afford to have a nose that is likely to keep on growing until she can swallow it.

Fanny Brice, regarding her nose-job

I already have enough cosmetics in my bathroom to make up every single extra in *The Ten Commandments*.

Jean Kerr

I've always had a strong Kabuki streak.

Diana Vreeland

In high school my acne was so bad, blind people tried to read my face.

Joan Rivers

Appearances

Her mouth was the most voluptuous red thing in mouths, and much too large for beauty. She would have looked downright bad but her eyes — dewy hyacinths set in a forest of coarse jet firs. They said all sorts of things to people — especially men.

Elinor Glyn, describing Ava Cleveland

Beauty is neither wholly the gift of God nor the gift of the cosmetician.

Helena Rubinstein

BREASTS

My feet are small for the same reason my waist is small — things don't grow in the shade.

Dolly Parton

When we consider the significant cultural shifts of the past few years, the removal of Pamela Anderson's breast implants must rank right up there at the top.

Suzanne Moore

Girls got balls. They're just a little higher up, that's all.

Joan Jett

Mrs Foote had ... several black moles on her face and breasts so big if they had hands at the end of them they might be useful.

Jane Hamilton

[God] wouldn't have given them to me if he hadn't wanted people to notice them.

Dolly Parton

BOTTOMS

There's a broad with a future behind her.
Constance Bennett on beholding Marilyn Monroe's rear end

To me, though, the symbol of Switzerland is that large middle class female behind. It is the most respectable thing in the world. It is deathless. Everyone has one in this hotel; some of the elderly ladies have two.

Katherine Mansfield

HAIR

As for blondes having more fun, well, let me dispel that rumour forever. They do.

Maureen Lipman

The woman with big hair is not remotely interested in looking fawnlike, as Mia Farrow does, but rather in looking as if she could eat little Mia for breakfast.

India Knight

The great question — what do people DO for fun in countries where there are no blondes?

Paula Yates

Appearances

The look I have gone for is so fake blonde, it's practically mocking.

Emma Forrest

Where I come from a woman who dyes her hair when it is beginning to turn grey is considered as good as lost.

Edna Ferber

My God, I'm outliving my henna.

Red-haired American comedienne Lucille Ball, then in her eighties

My memories of school have every girl in the class, except me, as blonde and pale as glasses of milk. This may explain my irrational, yet heartfelt hatred of Gwyneth Paltrow.

Emma Forrest

I've been very pleased with my hair on occasions. At least it doesn't usually give me cause for abject despair as the rest of me often does. Possibly because by the time it's grown, it's dead.

Maureen Lipman

I'm not offended by all the dumb-blonde jokes because I know that I'm not dumb. I also know I'm not blonde.

Dolly Parton

Every time I hear some smooth voice-over on a hair advertisement say, "It's really important to have healthy shiny hair", I think, not if you look like the back of a bus it ain't.

Jo Brand

AGE

I am not so nice as I was, but I am nicer than Rose Macaulay
— also she is a spindle shanked withered virgin: I never felt
anyone so utterly devoid of the sexual parts.

Virginia Woolf

He was there with two very worn and chipped looking
ladies — the saddest looking remnants of ladies — in fact
they reminded me of those cups without saucers that you
sometimes see outside a china shop — all-on-this-tray-one-
penny.

Katherine Mansfield

Your friends, wherever they may be, say, "Darling, you looked
ten years younger."

And you say to yourself, "That's all very well, but I wanted
to look fifteen years younger."

Beatrice Lillie on being on television

I manage to look so young because I'm mentally retarded.

Debbie Harry

My body is falling so fast, my gynaecologist wears a hard hat.

Joan Rivers

I was there [at the beauty parlour] five hours — and that was
just for the estimate.

Phyllis Diller

Appearances

Take a close-up of a woman past sixty! You might as well use a picture of a relief map of Ireland!

Nancy Astor, when asked for a close-up photograph

After fifty you have to deserve your face.

Coco Chanel

Just because my anatomy has been rearranged several times by natural disasters, childbirth and some cooking accidents doesn't mean I can't give advice as well as Jane, Linda and other beautiful stars.

Phyllis Diller

As far as I am concerned, age does not exist. I know twenty-year-old girls who are older than me.

Zsa Zsa Gabor

I also saw Mademoiselle d'Épernon, who thought me a little altered; we had not seen each other for upwards of thirty years. How horribly changed she seemed to be.

Marie de Sévigné

If the Nobel Prize was awarded by a woman, it would go to the inventor of the dimmer switch.

Kathy Lette

How come I'm reading articles with names like A Woman's Guide to Cosmetic Surgery more than I'm reading the poems of Dylan Thomas?

Judith Viorst

At least, she is not any worse-looking than she used to be in
her youth; hers are features which never alter, unfortunately
for her.

George Sand

Being over seventy is rather like being Royalty. The luxuries
that become yours by right are incredible, but the penalties
are extreme.

Rachel Ferguson

If you want to see some scared women, hang out in
Houston, Beverly Hills, or Palm Beach, and watch those girls
hit forty.

Rita Mae Brown

I have been asked to pose for *Penthouse* on my hundredth
birthday. Everybody is going to be sorry.

Dolly Parton

MODELS

In the old days a model was simply a model; she broke men's
hearts but not their traditions.

Djuna Barnes

I always like to compare models to supermodels in the way I
compare Tampax to Super Tampax: supermodels cost a bit
more and they are a lot thicker.

Jo Brand

Appearances

A sex symbol becomes a thing. I just hate being a thing. But if I'm going to be a symbol of something, I'd rather have it sex than some other things we've got symbols of.

Marilyn Monroe

CLOTHES

The contents of a handbag, like good whisky in a charred oak barrel, ripen and improve with age.

Peg Bracken

Doctors … are against all sorts of femininities — high heels, tight clothing, false eyelashes.

Germaine Greer

It is almost as stupid to let your clothes betray that you know you are ugly as to have them proclaim that you think you are beautiful.

Edith Wharton

Clothes do not actually influence availability. If all that stands between a male chauvinist and the accomplishment of his desires is a knicker, then you've had it.

Germaine Greer

I can remember when pants were pants. You wore them for twenty years, then you cut them down for pan scrubs. Or quilts.

Victoria Wood

Appearances

I like fashion to go down into the street, but I can't accept that it should originate there.

Coco Chanel

Elegance is refusal.

Diana Vreeland

There's comfort to an awful old dressing-gown a pretty *peignoir* is powerless to provide, and aging bra elastic, is, I suspect, as near to liberation as most women ever get.

Katharine Whitehorn

[Madame de Soubise] has been silly enough to dip deep with the silk mercer, but she would have done better had she spent part of her money in something else; as it is impossible to buy a new face, dress is thrown away upon her.

Marie de Sévigné

You can be better dressed when you own a lot of stuff.

Helen Gurley Brown

After being known as the biggest frump in America and Europe, I am now the world's oldest stylish stout.

Elsa Maxwell

It is the old adjective game, and we reserve the prettiest words for ourselves. (I'm casual; you're messy; she's a slob.)

Peg Bracken

Appearances

Only fifty per cent of men believe the way to a man's heart is through his stomach. Food is therefore less important than wearing a black dress.

Elizabeth Hawes

I'm not one for dance classes, feeling if God had wanted us to wear leotards he would have painted us purple.

Victoria Wood

The bikini is the most important invention since the atom bomb.

Diana Vreeland

[The New Woman] cannot resist the squaw-like preference for animals' skins, and slaughtered birds, and tufts torn out of the living and bleeding creature.

Ouida

Now, if you're short-legged, very short skirts won't make you look long-legged, just cold.

Peg Bracken

Her crimson dress, exaggerated like all the rest in this strange picture, hung about her in folds which looked like flames, her fair head peeping out of the lurid mass of colour as if out of a raging furnace.

Mary Braddon

Appearances

The Brandon family at the present moment have got their Sunday faces and their Sunday clothes on, and they misbecome most of them very sorely.

Rhoda Broughton

You mean those clothes of hers are intentional?

Dorothy Parker

Lady Dolly ought to have been perfectly happy. She had everything that can constitute the joys of a woman of her epoch. She was at Trouville. She had won heaps of money at play. She had made a correct book on the races. She had seen her chief rival looking bilious in an unbecoming gown.

Ouida

Don't you think fashion is basically over?

Cynthia Heimel

May's bonnet is a sight for gods and men. Black and white outside, with a great cockade boiling over the front to meet a red ditto surging from the interior, where a red rainbow darts across the brow, and a surf of white lace foams up on each side. I expect to hear that you and John fell flat in the dust with horror on beholding it.

Louisa May Alcott

Hats divide generally into three classes: offensive hats, defensive hats, and shrapnel.

Katharine Whitehorn

Appearances

Yes, your bonnet is delicious, darling; and though the
diminutive size of that velvet jacket would lead me to
suppose you had borrowed it from a juvenile sister, it seems
the very garment of all garments best calculated to render
you just one hair's-breadth nearer perfection than you were
made by nature.

Mary Braddon

I've seen women turn actually grey under the weight of their
tiaras.

Gertrude Atherton

She is dressed with rigid simplicity; certainly paler, and, if
possible, neater than ever, the little bunch of snowdrops she
wears completing the picture of almost awful chastity which
she presents.

Rhoda Broughton

There is many a lonely heart beating beneath a diamond
parure.

Mary Dunn

"White is so very trying," she said, as if Daphne's were not a
beauty that could afford to be tried.

Mary Braddon

[The New Woman] cannot go into the country without
making herself a caricature of a man, in coat and waistcoat
and gaiters; she apes all his absurdities, she emulates all his
cruelties and follies.

Ouida

Their dress is very independent of fashion; as they observe,
"What does it signify how we dress at Cranford, where
everybody knows us?" And if they go from home, their
reason is equally cogent: "What does it signify how we dress
here, where nobody knows us?"

Mrs Gaskell

Dress designing, incidentally, is to me not a profession but an
art.

Elsa Schiaparelli

Art, conceived as dressmaking, is a pretentious cloak I'll
never wear, it wouldn't suit me.

Gabrielle Chanel

I think genius in dressmaking principally consists of inventing
in the summer dresses for winter; and in the winter inventing
dresses for summer. That is difficult enough, believe me,
without dragging in aesthetics or the sublime.

Gabrielle Chanel

TARTS

A woman can look both moral and exciting — if she also
looks as if it was quite a struggle.

Edna Ferber

When she raises her eyelids it's as if she were taking off all
her clothes.

Colette

You show me a woman with a naturally beautiful body, and I'll show you a tramp!

Joan Rivers

Today, wannabes, already-ams and have-beens compete to be noticed more for what they don't wear than what they do.

Jane Moore

It costs a lot to make a person look this cheap.

Dolly Parton

I may look sweet but I wear leather underwear.

Spice Girl Emma Bunton

A female sloven is an odious sight.

Charlotte Yonge

I am the original Sex Symbol. The others are counterfeit.

Mae West

The hair is white blonde, the roots thick and dark, and the cut so choppy it doesn't say "Come to bed" so much as "I haven't been to bed".

Emma Forrest

SPECIFIC

The Prince, for we met them often walking about, was exactly like hundreds of other young men, fair & gentlemanly enough, about one & twenty. She was much taller and walked very badly, enormous long steps and about twenty-seven I should think & fine looking, but her bonnet completely spoiled her face and was most extraordinary, being of cased blue velvet but the shape was truly frightful. It was exactly as if you had taken the centre of your bonnet & made it touch your forehead, in this way [a drawing] and the face very far back so you could hardly see it.

Effie Ruskin

I have seen scarecrows that did credit to farmers' boys' ingenuity, but never one better calculated to scare all birds, beasts and human beings.

Mary Bull on Susan B. Anthony

Why did he [Onassis] marry that Jackie? She is ugly, with horrible legs, the skin of a hen, fat in the wrong places, and eyes too far apart from one another. She's a big nothing.

Lisa Calogeropoulos, mother of Maria Callas, former mistress of Aristotle Onassis

He didn't need to take a change of shoes. He can always wear hers. She has very big feet, you know.

Vivien Merchant, referring to her husband, Harold Pinter, leaving her for Lady Antonia Fraser

Appearances

... Katie like a bit of a Greek temple lying in the grass —
and Beatrice a gargoyle come to life!
Virginia Woolf on the daughters of the Marchioness of Bath

Poor dear pretty Siddons! What has she been doing to her
mouth? Picking it, my master says, as I do my fingers, which,
he threatens me, are one day to resemble poor Mr
Pennington's toes. But in earnest and true sadness, what can
be the matter with her lips? Lips that never were equalled in
enunciation of tenderness or sublimity! Lips that spoke so
kindly to me and of me! Dear soul! what can ail her? She
dreamed once that all her teeth came out upon the stage I
remember; I told her she would go on acting till age had
bereft her of them.
Hester Thrale on the actress Sarah Siddons

She is a horrible looking woman — looks as horrible as she
is. I was going to say that she looks like an epitome of the
Seven Sins. But that would be paying her a compliment —
imputing to her a certain greatness. There is no greatness.
She is just an open slum.
Edith Sitwell on Leonor Fini, an Italian painter and set designer

It [her beauty] may be natural, but it looks like affectation.
The Honourable Emily Eden

Women like Mrs Keppel ... suck up all the Technicolor in a
room and leave other women stranded in Kansas.
Liesl Schillinger

Both George Eliot and Lewes were singularly
unencumbered with personal attractions.

Julia Clara Byrne

Julie de Lespinasse was now twenty-two and formed both in
mind and body. She had every quality which made for
beauty, and yet she was not pretty. Perhaps she might have
been considered prettier if her head had been larger. For no
feature could show to full advantage in the small amount of
space available in such a little head.

Thérèse L Latour

The Princess was one of those women who are all the more
dangerous for not being beautiful.

Julia Clara Byrne on the Princess de Lieven

Nature did her best to make Mrs— a very charming
woman, only poor Nature was sadly thwarted.

Geraldine Endsor Jewsbury

I apparently remind some people of their mother-in-law or
their boss, or something.

Hillary Rodham Clinton

Amelia's beauty is one of those delusions I have never given
into.

The Honourable Emily Eden

Appearances

There were very few Beauties, & such as there were, were not very handsome. Miss Iremonger did not look well, & Mrs Blount was the only one much admired. She appeared exactly as she did in September, with the same broad face, diamond bandeau, white shoes, pink husband, & fat neck.

Jane Austen

But Miss Pix had that air of arrested development peculiar to the best statuary. Her skin was as white as the tablecloth, her profile was mathematically straight, suggesting an antique marble or a sheep.

Gertrude Atherton

Now to me, Edith looks like something that would eat her young.

Dorothy Parker

She is so hairy — when she lifted up her arm, I thought it was Tina Turner in her armpit.

Joan Rivers on Madonna

Did you see that girl come out? Her face is like an evil flower. She has a slash of rouge for a mouth. She's so intense she vibrates.

Jane Cowl on Tallulah Bankhead

She looked more like a German *hausfrau* than a glamour queen. Her clothes were almost as funny as some I'd seen before leaving Altoona; only Marlene's cost more.

Hedda Hopper on Marlene Dietrich

Her skin had the pure cold whiteness of the camellia; and her admirers swore that her feet and hands necessitated a magnifying glass.

Gertrude Atherton

Those eyebrows wound up looking like African caterpillars!

Bette Davis on Joan Crawford

MEN

He was so ugly he hurt my feelings.

Jackie "Moms" Mabley

The softer a man's head, the louder his socks.

Helen Rowland

Look at man in the light of a shell fish and he will certainly come off worst in terms of beauty and design of his architecture.

George Eliot

Men's physical beauty has now become as rare as their moral beauty has always been.

Louise Colet

Appearances

We hear of a young lady exclaiming, at the prospect of marriage, "How awful it must be, to be seen by one's husband — in — one's petticoats!" ... There was a bride who wrote home to her mamma that she was horrified by the sight of her husband's night-shirts; and that she was spending the honeymoon "making him nice long night-gowns so that I shan't be able to see any of him".

Phyllis Cunnington

HAIR

I don't know why they call it Grecian 2000, like if Socrates (who was Grecian) was still alive today, in his cave, he'd have a lovely mop of shiny black hair ...

Helen Stevenson

I love bald men. Just because you've lost your fuzz, don't mean you ain't a peach.

Dolly Parton

CLOTHES

I want to know why, if men rule the world, they don't stop wearing neckties.

Linda Ellerbee

When a woman looks at a man in evening dress, she sometimes can't help wondering why he wants to blazon his ancestry to the world by wearing a coat with a long tail to it.

Helen Rowland

Appearances

During the season white duck trousers used to be much worn by gentlemen in the park, and the extreme tightness which fashion at one time prescribed for these occasionally led to some ludicrous incidents.

Lady Dorothy Nevill

Look at man's uniform drabness, his impersonal envelope! ...The drape of the male is designed to achieve self-forgetfulness.

Carolyn Kizer

SPECIFIC MEN

Naturally she had her son Randall along. He was so fat if he sat on a worm on a rock it would make a fossil in about five minutes. Then scientists wouldn't have to wait a million years.

Jane Hamilton

The dear beast of a man is so filthy, frightful, odious and detestable I would turn away such a footman for fear of spoiling my dinner while he waited at table.

Lady Mary Wortley Montagu

At a New York party ... Tallulah Bankhead pointed to the actor and said, in a loud voice, "look how ugly he is!" And when Laughton died, Tallulah's only comment was, "he had such dirty nails".

Tallulah Bankhead on Charles Laughton

His hair contrived to collect more dust than the usual laws of capillary attraction warranted. His black neckcloth turned browner and hung looser than common black cravats; his coat was a dingy brown — and, altogether, he had the air of an exhausted ink-bottle.

The Honourable Emily Eden

Mr Tremore was one of the most unsightly lovers that ever aspired to bear the name. He was of a huge circumference, and what is unusual in persons of that make, he was a mass of rancour and malevolence — gifted however with a wit so keen and deadly, that with its razor edge, he cut to the heart most of his enemies, and all his friends.

Lady Caroline Lamb

The style and dash of the eighties had passed him by.

Isla Dewar

Churchill wasn't as tubby then as he is today, but with his round pink cheeks he did look like a mature cherub.

Hedda Hopper on Winston Churchill